STUDIES IN ENGLISH LITERATURE

Volume CIII

SHELLEY
AND NONVIOLENCE

by

ART YOUNG

Michigan Technological University

1975
MOUTON
THE HAGUE · PARIS

Mouton & Co. N.V., Publishers, The Hague
© Copyright 1975 in The Netherlands

ISBN   90 279 3031 7

76-355879

Printed in The Netherlands

CONTENTS

for Ann

I
INTRODUCTION

> Lord, enlighten thou our enemies, sharpen their
> wits, give acuteness to their perceptions, and
> consecutiveness and clearness to their reasoning
> powers, we are in danger from their folly, not
> from their wisdom; their weakness is what fills
> us with apprehension, not their strength.
>
> John Stuart Mill

The struggle for human liberties through nonviolence is a movement that has gained increasing momentum in the twentieth century. Percy Bysshe Shelley was the first English writer to recommend in his poetry massive civil disobedience and organized passive resistance as nonviolent tactics for social reform. But his contribution to nonviolent philosophy extends beyond the implications found in his famous "The Mask of Anarchy" to a coherent philosophy of action that can be recognized as playing a prominent role in this Romantic poet's philosophical, political, and ethical thought. This study will attempt to demonstrate that one of the primary purposes of Shelley's writings is to inspire men to nonviolently combat injustice, and that his choice in promulgating nonviolence as the major ethical and practical means of reform was the result of conscious conviction and a well-developed, rational philosophy, a philosophy that can be witnessed throughout the writings of this socially-minded poet and political pamphleteer. I will attempt to define Shelley's nonviolent philosophy through an analysis of his poetry, drama, and prose. In an age when nuclear holocaust threatens to extinguish the human race, Shelley's very real contribution to imaginative nonviolent thought needs to be pondered.

Generally speaking, nonviolent thought as it appears in the works of Shelley can be divided into a series of corresponding dualities for the sake of discussion and understanding, although in actuality the corresponding components are usually mutually inclusive. Shelley's preference for nonviolent action to combat injustice, as opposed to either violent action or inaction, is both ethically and pragmatically grounded in his imaginative and rational faith in humanity. Ethically Shelley believed that violence is wrong because it corrupts the individual soul that it is supposedly attempting to liberate, and pragmatically it is unwise because it gives social acceptability to those destructive impulses in human nature that in themselves deny the possibility of peace and brotherhood. Shelley desired not only that the evils of an unjust political system be eliminated, but also that men participate in a revolution of consciousness – on one level to make nonviolence instead of violence the acceptable method of resolving conflicts – in order to insure the establishment and continuation of a just society.

Shelley's philosophy of action includes reform of the individual seeking to lead a better life, and reform of the state whose purpose should be to provide a better life for its people. To the individual, nonviolence is a way of life, an attempt at self-purification, that is, the elimination of fear and the products of fear, violence and hatred from self, and the infusion of love and the products of love, truth and justice, in self. Collective nonviolent action is the gathering together of individuals to actively protest the existence of a social injustice in their society, or to instigate the reform of a political institution. In an attempt to make justice prevail, collective nonviolent action includes the use of noncooperation, civil disobedience, passive resistance, and commitment to meaningful reform within the established system. In both cases, individual and collective, the nonviolent activist seeks to realize courage and fortitude through suffering love and to make a strategic weapon of forgiveness.

The artistic presentation of Shelley's vision of nonviolence includes imaginatively glorifying the grandeur and courage of nonviolent action as in *The Revolt of Islam* and *Prometheus Unbound*, and realistically portraying the horror and futility of violence as in *The Cenci* and *Hellas*. Shelley consistently attempted to make his readers exercise their moral imaginations in order to create a better world; he desired to make brotherly love an agent of reform. And although he frequently shifted the artistic perspective of his vision of truth, his approach to the conflict between good and evil within and without man changed little from his early "Address to the Irish People" until his final, uncompleted *The Triumph of Life*.

1

Popular conceptions of Shelley's political thought as interpreted from his poetry and prose have tended to divide into two polarized camps: one camp maintains that Shelley was an ethereal idealist, whose political and social thoughts and prophecies, although admirable, are visionary and unrealistic; the other camp proclaims with equal assurance that Shelley was a sensitive poetic spirit who wasted his poetic sensibility on an anarchistic and potentially dangerous political philosophy. But there has always been a segment of critics, from Shelley's contemporary Leigh Hunt[1] to Henry Salt[2] and other early members of the *Shelley Society,* and scholars such as A. Stanley Walker[3] and Carl Grabo[4] in this century, who have attempted to demonstrate the rationality and practicality of his specific programs for reform and the authenticity and validity of his poetic vision of mankind's potential to establish a just and peaceful society. While Shelley's aversion to violence and his pleas for peaceful reform have been well documented by even his most hostile critics, it has only been recently that scholars have attempted to see a coherent philosophy of nonviolence in Shelley's

[1] See *The Autobiography of Leigh Hunt* (London: Cresset Press, 1949), and Hunt's reviews of Shelley's works in *The Unextinguished Hearth* (Durham: Duke University Press, 1938) by Newman Ivey White.
[2] See Salt's *Percy Bysshe Shelley: Poet and Pioneer* (1896; rpt.: Port Washington, New York: Kennikat Press, 1968).
[3] See Walker's "Peterloo, Shelley, and Reform", *Publications of the Modern Language Association,* XL (1925), 128-64.
[4] See Grabo's *The Magic Plant: The Growth of Shelley's Thought* (Chapel Hill: University of North Carolina Press, 1936).

political vision. The genesis for my study originated when I heard Professor Roland Duerksen give a speech on nonviolence and Shelley at Miami University in the spring of 1969. Moreover, Professor Duerksen, in addition to his helpful *Shelleyan Ideas in Victorian Literature* (1966),[5] has published a preface to *The Cenci*[6] and a preface to Shelley's political writings[7] in which he has emphasized the nonviolent elements in Shelley's works. His "Preface" to *Shelley: Political Writings* begins,

Readers who know Percy Bysshe Shelley as the author of "To a Skylark," "Indian Serenade," and other frequently anthologized poems may be startled to learn that in his sensitivity to, and his articulate enthusiasm for, social reform he anticipated and challenged later radicals. Some groups of political activists today appear motivated by the same inner urgency that impelled Shelley. In all English literature, Shelley was one of the first prophetic voices of a movement which in the twentieth century has attained vast proportions in the struggle for human rights and individual dignity – a movement for nonviolent reform that some observers believe could yet become a worldwide alternative to nuclear destruction.[8]

In addition to Professor Roland Duerksen's works, numerous publications on Shelley by other scholars, some hostile, some reverential, have been extremely helpful to me in my attempt to comprehend the role that nonviolence plays in Shelley's political thought. The various articles of Kenneth Neill Cameron[9] and his pioneer work *The Young Shelley*[10] were especially useful in relating Shelley to the social movements of his time and in providing the historical and contemporary allusions which form the necessary framework for many of Shelley's works. Although Professor Cameron is sometimes too insistent on the political interpretations of Shelley's writings at the expense of the varied richness of mean-

---

[5]   *Shelleyan Ideas in Victorian Literature* (The Hague: Mouton, 1966).
[6]   *The Cenci* (New York: Bobbs-Merrill Company, Inc., 1970).
[7]   *Shelley: Political Writings* (New York: Appleton-Century-Crofts, 1970).
[8]   *Shelley: Political Writings*, vii.
[9]   "The Political Symbolism of Prometheus Unbound", *Publications of the Modern Language Association*, LVIII (1943), 728-53; "Shelley and the Reformers", *Journal of English Literary History*, XII (1945), 62-86; and "The Social Philosophy of Shelley", *Sewanee Review*, L (1942), 457-66.
[10]   *The Young Shelley: Genesis of a Radical* (New York: Macmillan Company, 1950).

ing and experience to be found in them, he is to be credited for the extent to which his work has countered the all-too-accepted thesis of Arnold and Eliot that Shelley was "ineffectual", and to which it has begun a revaluation of Shelley as an ethical and political thinker.

Three recent book-length studies dealing with Shelley's political thought should be mentioned. Gerald McNiece in his book *Shelley and the Revolutionary Idea* (1969) demonstrates how the historical pattern of revolution operates in Shelley's works.[11] His book deals more with the fact of revolution than with the Shelleyan means, and as a result McNiece interprets Shelley's willingness to accept gradual reform as minimizing his revolutionary idealism. The two levels at which Shelleyan ideas operate are understood better, perhaps, by McNiece's anonymous reviewer in the *Times Literary Supplement,* who writes,

The immediate practical side of Shelley was directed to current politics and the reform of Establishment evils. At the upper end of the same register stands the Titan Prometheus, symbol of man's creative vision, with Asia, representing the ultimate requirement for regeneration – universal love. Shelley, himself a "Titan," could sound the two voices separately or together, aware of them as parts of the one harmony.[12]

Professor McNiece sees the later Shelley as near despair – his earlier confidence in humanity's ability to reform itself severely diminished.

Shelley's Political Thought (1969) by John Pollard Guinn is an analytical survey of Shelley's political writings.[13] Although Professor Guinn does not deal extensively with the role of nonviolence in Shelley's political thought, he does appreciatively recognize it: "He [Shelley] saw more clearly, perhaps, than any of his contemporaries the futility of violence as a means of securing reform."[14] After acknowledging the similarity between Shelley's thought and that of Gandhi, Guinn in the concluding five or six

---

[11] *Shelley and the Revolutionary Idea* (Cambridge, Massachusetts: Harvard University Press, 1969).
[12] July 23, 1970 (No. 3, 569).
[13] *Shelley's Political Thought* (The Hague: Mouton, 1969).
[14] *Shelley's Political Thought*, 12.

pages of his book deals with the possible influence of Shelley on
Gandhi, and his analysis will be discussed in the next chapter.

Carl Woodring devotes the longest section of his book *Politics
in English Romantic Poetry* (1970) to Shelley.[15] Concerning the
Romantics' contribution (including Shelley's) to political thought,
Woodring concludes,

Politically, the romantics contributed most to later generations in
deepening the liberal ideal. They introduced into poetry and life a
sense – too variable from one poet to another to be called an idea –
of imagination as the sympathetic movement from self into others.[16]

Woodring, like McNiece, sees Shelley in his later works compro-
mising his earlier idealism and revolutionary ardor; he even goes
so far as to declare that Shelley's alleged compromise with idealism was also an abandoning of his earlier pacifism. Shelley's
sympathetic change in attitude toward Christianity, according to
Woodring, "goes hand in glove with his acceptance of violence
as the means of securing independence".[17]

For my investigation of writers among Shelley's voluminous
reading who may have influenced his political vision, and especially his nonviolent philosophy, I have found particularly helpful,
in addition to Cameron, Newman Ivey White's two volume biography of Shelley[18] and David Lee Clark's excellent "Introduction" and "Notes" to his edition of Shelley's prose.[19] Of significant value because of its extensive investigation of anti-war sentiment and discussion of pacifism in the late seventeen hundreds,
especially among the early English Romantic poets, Blake, Wordsworth, Coleridge, and Southey, is Roland Bartel's unpublished
dissertation "Anti-War Sentiment in the Late Eighteenth Century".[20] Bartel concludes his study with an epilogue on "The Pacifism of Shelley" in which he states that "in many respects Shelley's attitude toward war is a poetic fusion of the best elements

[15] *Politics in English Romantic Poetry* (Cambridge, Massachusetts: Harvard University Press, 1970).
[16] *Politics . . .*, 330.
[17] *Politics . . .*, 317.
[18] *Shelley* (New York: Alfred A. Knopf, 1940).
[19] *Shelley's Prose* (Albuquerque: University of New Mexico Press, 1956).
[20] Indiana University, 1951.

of the writings against war in the seventeen-nineties".[21]

Other commentators on Shelley, although their works are not specifically concerned with Shelley's political thought, include Ellsworth Barnard, *Shelley's Religion* (1937), Carlos Baker, *Shelley's Major Poetry* (1948), Harold Bloom, *Shelley's Mythmaking* (1959) and *The Visionary Company* (1961), and Earl Wasserman, *Shelley's Prometheus Unbound* (1965).[22] Each of these scholars acknowledges with varying degrees of emphasis Shelley's commitment to the fundamental principles of nonviolence – principles we will define in Shelleyan terms as we analyze Shelley at work in defining them for himself.

2

Nonviolence does not simply mean the absence of violence. Nonviolence is not a passive state, but an intensively active force. In attempting to define the term *nonviolence* as it will be used in this study, and as I interpret Gandhi conceived its meaning and Shelley comprehended it, the key words are truth and love, will and imagination, suffering and forgiveness. Gandhi, not at all pleased with the negative and passive connotations of the word *nonviolence*, preferred the Hindu word *satyagraha* which he translated "truth-force" or "soul-force".

Satyagraha is literally holding on to Truth and it means, therefore, Truth-force. Truth is soul or spirit. It is therefore, known as soulforce. It excludes the use of violence because man is not capable of knowing the absolute truth and, therefore, not competent to punish.[23]

Truth and love (Gandhi's *ahimsa*) are the eternal qualities from which the nonviolent activist derives his power. In one very real

[21] "Anti-War Sentiment", 258.
[22] *Shelley's Religion* (Minneapolis: University of Minnesota Press, 1937); *Shelley's Major Poetry* (Princeton: Princeton University Press, 1948); *Shelley's Mythmaking* (New Haven: Yale University Press, 1959); *The Visionary Company* (Garden City, New York: Doubleday & Company, Inc., 1961); *Shelley's Prometheus Unbound* (Baltimore: Johns Hopkins Press, 1965).
[23] M. K. Gandhi, *Non-Violent Resistance* (New York: Schocken Books, 1969), 3.

sense they represent the ceaseless striving after Godhead; truth and love are but different faces of the nonviolent coin. Will and imagination are the human qualities by which men pursue love and truth. The imagination to move from self into others and the will to suffer yourself rather than inflict suffering on others are the backbone of the nonviolent activist's courage and endurance. "There is no love where there is no will."[24] The courage of the nonviolent soldier surpasses that of the violent one – for it is courage inspired by love rather than by fear. It is the courage of Shelley's Prometheus, of Socrates and Christ, of Mahandas Gandhi and Martin Luther King.

Suffering voluntarily undergone and forgiveness of those who cause suffering are the basic, strategic weapons of nonviolence; nonviolence is always willing to accept honorable compromise with an opponent, but recognizes that ultimate victory comes only with the conversion of all parties to truth and justice. Nonviolence is truth and the act of seeking truth. Suffering love seeks to attack the moral fiber of men in an attempt to persuade; it seeks through dynamic, nonviolent, human interaction to create understanding and love. Suffering plays the same role in a nonviolent movement that it plays in an artistic work such as Shelley's *The Cenci*; it makes the observers sensitive to morality, sensitive to considerations of justice.[25] The weapons of the non-violent militant are within him, and are as refined and sophisticated as the strength of his fire-tempered will.

Nonviolence is distinguished from *violence* in that it is in itself a forceful power, while violence is an agent of power. Nonviolence is the opposite of violence in the sense that self-suffering is the opposite of violence. Truth and love are the first casualties of the violent. Instead of loving an enemy and desiring eternal life in truth for him, it seeks to destroy him, it seeks to turn men into things. Joan Bondurant's simplified definitions may be of help to us here:

[24] M. K. Gandhi, quoted by Erik H. Erikson, *Gandhi's Truth* (New York: W. W. Norton & Company, Inc., 1969), 290.
[25] Joan Bondurant makes a similar point. *Conquest of Violence: The Gandhian Philosophy of Conflict* (Los Angeles: University of California Press, 1969), 229.

Force I take to mean the exercise of physical or intangible power or influence to effect change. *Violence* is the willful application of force in such a way that it is intentionally injurious to the person or group against whom it is applied. *Injury* is understood to include psychological as well as physical harm. *Non-violence* when used in connection with satyagraha means the exercise of power or influence to effect change without injury to the opponent.[26]

"Love never claims, it ever gives. Love ever suffers, never resents, never revenges itself."[27]

Pacifism can be considered as similar to nonviolence if pacifism is defined as an active, aggressive force seeking in the pursuit of truth the elimination of social injustices, and not simply defined as a moral position whereby the pacifist refuses to participate in violence. But one important distinction between the pacifist and the nonviolent philosopher should be mentioned at this point, and will be discussed in greater detail later. The pacifist believes that all violence is wrong, and as a matter of conscience refuses to support the violence of either party in a violent conflict. On the other hand, the nonviolent militant in both Shelley's and Gandhi's philosophy, although he himself recognizes the inherent evil of violence, also recognizes the relativity involved in each man's approach to this moral issue, and therefore he may support the violent efforts of those who would eliminate injustice. Thus Shelley enthusiastically supported the Greek and Italian efforts to overthrow the tyrannies that oppressed them, and Gandhi formed an ambulance corps in the British service during World War I in support of their cause.

Passive resistance, non-cooperation, and *civil disobedience* are strategic, physical weapons of nonviolence. They are physical because they require physical acts of nonviolence. Gandhi disliked the term *passive resistance* because it "has been conceived and is regarded as a weapon of the weak"[28] in which violent response to oppression is forsaken because of weakness and fear of retaliation, and thus passivity becomes the logical and sometimes cowardly choice. In this sense it is incompatible with

---

[26] *Conquest of Violence,* 9.
[27] M. K. Gandhi, quoted by Bondurant, 26.
[28] *Non-Violent Resistance,* 3.

nonviolence. But in the sense that I will use the term, one recognized as valid by Gandhi,[29] passive resistance is a forceful act of "truth-force" in which resisters fearlessly confront injustice, usually collectively, and courageously refuse to be intimidated by threats of reprisal, violent or otherwise.

Non-cooperation is the positive act of refusing to cooperate with a system of government which "in the non-cooperator's view has become corrupt".[30] To continue in Gandhi's words,

Non-co-operation is not a passive state, it is an intensely active state – more active than physical resistance or violence. Passive resistance is a misnomer. Non-co-operation in the sense used by me must be non-violent and, therefore, neither punitive nor vindicative nor based on malice, ill-will or hatred.[31]

Civil disobedience is a more direct and selective form of non-co-operation. An act of civil disobedience by nonviolent resisters is the deliberate violation of an unjust law and the willingness to cheerfully suffer, as a testament to the resister's sincerity, the consequences under law which might result.

Non-co-operation and civil disobedience are but different branches of the same tree called Satyagraha. It is my *Kalpadruma* – my *Jam-i-Jam* – the Universal Provider. Satyagraha is search for Truth; and God is Truth. *Ahimsa* or nonviolence is the light that reveals that Truth to me.[32]

3

In the succeeding chapters I will attempt to define and analyze Shelley's nonviolent philosophy as it can be seen in a selective group of his writings. I have chosen works of Shelley from all stages of his career and from the various genres within which he worked which have special reference to his political thought and nonviolent philosophy. Chapter Two will be devoted to comparing some of the numerous similarities between the philosophy of

---

[29] *Non-Violent Resistance*, 54.
[30] *Non-Violent Resistance*, 4.
[31] *Non-Violent Resistance*, 161-62.
[32] *Non-Violent Resistance*, 176.

nonviolence as expressed in the writings of Shelley and that expressed in the writings of Gandhi. The purpose of such a comparison will be to produce a framework from within which to examine Shelley's insights into the problem of human violence, as well as to enrich our understanding of nonviolence as defined by both these reformers. In the following chapters I will examine works of Shelley in roughly chronological order. "An Address to the Irish People" (1812) is one of Shelley's earliest works, and because of its elaborate presentation of Shelley's sense of social injustice, of altruism, of responsible and responsive government, and of nonviolent methods of reform, it is a particularly profitable essay in which to establish those principles which generally guided Shelley throughout his brief life as a poet and concerned citizen of the world. *The Revolt of Islam* (1817) and *Prometheus Unbound* (1818-19) depict from radically different perspectives nonviolent revolutions. In both dramatic poems the hero turns from accepting revenge and violence as legitimate modes of human behavior to replacing them with the nonviolent principles of pity, forgiveness, and love. In *The Cenci* (1819) and *The Triumph of Life* (1822) Shelley examines violence and nonviolence from a realistic perspective, from a perspective that sees Beatrice Cenci fail where Prometheus has succeeded. Other works to be considered include "The Mask of Anarchy" (1819), "A Philosophical View of Reform" (1819), *Swellfoot the Tyrant* (1820), and *Hellas* (1821). In the summary chapter I will bring together some conclusions which can be drawn concerning the prominent place of nonviolence in Shelley's political and ethical thought.

II

SHELLEY AND GANDHI

> If you can avoid evil by suffering it yourself,
> do so. Try to help your enemy by overcoming
> him with kindness and meekness. If this does
> not help, then it is better that one perish than
> both of you. It is better that you be enriched
> with the advantage of patience than to render
> evil for evil. It is not enough to practice the
> golden rule in this matter. The greater your
> position the more ready you ought to be to
> forgive another's crime.
>
> Erasmus

> You [workingmen and laborers of Great Britain]
> are to do good work, whether you live or die.
> It may be that you will have to die; – well, men
> have died for their country often; be ready to
> die for her in doing her assured good: her, and
> all other countries with her. Mind your own
> business with absolute heart and soul; but see
> that it is good business first. That it is corn and
> sweet peas you are producing, – not gunpowder
> and arsenic. And be sure of this, literally: you
> must simply die rather than make any destroying
> mechanism or compound.
> There is no physical crime, at this day, so far
> beyond pardon, – so without parallel in its un-
> tempted guilt, as the making of war-machinery,
> and invention of mischievous substance. Two
> nations may go mad, and fight like harlots –
> God have mercy on them; – you, who hand
> them carving-knives off the table, for leave to
> pick up a dropped sixpence, what mercy is there
> for you?
>
> John Ruskin

This chapter will not be an extensive comparative analysis of

Shelley's and Gandhi's nonviolent philosophies, but rather it will suggest broad areas of similarity in the thinking of the two reformers. Such an effort is worthwhile if it contributes to defining patterns of thought in these two nonviolent activists, and if it stimulates the talents of other scholars to investigate the matter in greater depth. The influence of Indian thought on Shelley, and the influence of Shelley on Gandhi, are two areas that have not been investigated with any degree of thoroughness by critics. But there are two works on each subject which should be mentioned.

From the time of his friendship with Dr. Lind at Eaton and the access that he had to Dr. Lind's ample library, Shelley was attracted to Indian lore. Shelley's fascination with India continued to the end of his life; indeed, in the winter of 1821 he wrote to Peacock inquiring about the chances of going to live in India as an employee of the East India Company.[1] In his book entitled *Studies in Shelley,* Amiyakumar Sen has a chapter "Shelley and Indian Thought" in which he discusses the use Shelley makes of Indian images and symbols in his poetry, especially *Queen Mab,* "Alastor", *Prometheus Unbound,* and *Hellas.*[2] Sen also discusses the influence of Indian thought, which the poet gained second hand primarily through the works of Sir William Jones, on Shelley's philosophy. According to Sen, Hindu philosophical ideas as interpreted by Jones enabled Shelley to break with the Deistic tradition of the eighteenth century. Jones writes that the Hindus regarded the entire universe

rather as an *energy than a work,* by which the Infinite Being, who is present, at all times, in all places, exhibits to the minds of his creatures, a set of perceptions, like a wonderful picture or a piece of music, always varied yet always uniform, so that all bodies and their qualities exist, indeed, to every wise and useful purpose, but exist only so far as they are perceived.[3]

Sen concludes that Shelley discovered from the Hindu tradition that the "world of sense is thus a wondrous imagery woven by

[1] White, *Shelley,* II, 327.
[2] *Studies in Shelley* (1936; rpt.: Folcroft, Pennsylvania: Folcroft Press, Inc., 1969), 243-70.
[3] Sir William Jones as quoted by Sen, 253.

the pervading spirit. Its appearances are unsubstantial and they envelop ultimate reality as a veil."[4]

S.R. Swaminathan's article "Possible Indian Influence on Shelley" is similar to Sen's and provides interesting additional information.[5] Shelley's reading of Edward Moor's *Hindu Pantheon*, a work he is known to have ordered and received from his bookseller, may have helped him formulate his various symbols of the serpent and the eagle in combat, an image which is illustrated in Moor's book. In Hindu mythology the symbol of eternity is a huge serpent, and "evil, always pretending to be eternal and good, puts on the appearance of a serpent".[6] Thus the symbol of the serpent has ambiguous connotations in Hindu mythology, as it often does in Shelley's poetry. Swaminathan also emphasizes the importance of Sir William Jones' *Works* on the shaping of Shelley's mind. One selection from Jones in particular seems relevant to considerations of Shelley's "Alastor" and numerous other works in his canon.

The Vedantis and Sufis concur in believing that the souls of men differ infinitely in *degree*, but not at all in *kind*, from the divine spirit of which they are *particles*, and in which they will ultimately be absorbed. . . . that nothing has a pure absolute existence but *mind* or *spirit*; that material substances as the ignorant call them are no more than gay pictures presented continually to our minds by the sempiternal Artist; that we must beware of attachment to such *phantoms*, and attach ourselves exclusively to God, who truly exists in us, as we exist solely in Him; that we retain even in this forlorn state of separation from our beloved, the *idea of heavenly beauty* and the remembrance of our primeval vows; that sweet musick, gentle breezes, fragrant flowers perpetually renew the primary idea, refresh our fading memory, and melt us with tender affections.[7]

Early in his career Shelley in a letter to Elizabeth Hitchner declares that Southey's *Curse of Kehama*, a work which attempts to depict Indian life, is his "most favorite poem".[8] Considering

[4] Sen, 263.
[5] "Possible Indian Influence on Shelley", *Keats-Shelley Memorial Bulletin*, IX (1958), 30-45.
[6] "Possible Indian Influence . . .", 33.
[7] Sir William Jones as quoted by Swaminathan, 41.
[8] See Shelley's letter of June 11, 1811, to Miss Hitchner, *The Letters of Percy Bysshe Shelley*, ed. Frederick L. Jones, 2 vols. (Oxford: Clarendon

the enthusiasm that we know Shelley had for India, and considering the scholarship of Sen and Swaminathan, it seems viable to suggest that the Hindu philosophy which later so deeply influenced Gandhi may have also considerably influenced this Romantic poet in his search to construct a coherent philosophy of life. Indeed, the metaphysics of Shelley's nonviolence with its belief in a dynamic universe and the oneness of all life may have been formulated by his contact with Indian thought and then later enriched and confirmed by his subsequent reading of Plato and the New Testament.

On the other hand, there is no specific evidence available to demonstrate that Gandhi at the beginning of his career read any of Shelley's writings; however, there is evidence that Gandhi was in intimate contact with Shelleyan thought at the time when he was formulating his own philosophy of life. After reviewing the entire file of *Indian Opinion,* a periodical published by Gandhi, for the years 1903-1914, John Guinn concludes,

Judging from these facts concerning Gandhi's schooling and reading taste and habits and the fact that Shelley is not mentioned in any of the issues of *Indian Opinion*, we may safely conclude that he did not become acquainted with Shelley until sometime after 1914, the year which marked the end of his South African campaign.[9]

Geoffrey Ashe, whose biography of Gandhi was published a year earlier than Guinn's study of Shelley, but which was probably not available to Guinn before his book's completion, provides ample evidence that Gandhi as a young law student in England (1888-92) was frequently exposed to Shelley's ethical and political principles.[10] After arriving in England, Gandhi was profoundly moved by his reading of a series of vegetarian tracts by prominent Britishers. The most influential of these tracts was Henry Salt's *A Plea for Vegetarianism* in which food reform is related to reform of society in general. Shelley, Thoreau, and Ruskin are all appreciatively cited in support of Salt's plea for vegetarianism

---

Press, 1964), I, 246. All further references to Shelley's letters are to this edition, and will be given by Jones' numbering within the text.

[9] *Shelley's Political Thought*, 129.

[10] *Gandhi* (New York: Stein and Day, 1968), 29-40.

and social reform. At this time Gandhi also read Anna Kings-
ford's *The Perfect Way in Diet* and Howard Williams' *The Ethics
of Diet,* and as in Salt's pamphlet, he "encountered Shelley,
hymned . . . as an arch-prophet for the modern world".[11]

In the next year (1889) Gandhi became personally acquainted
with Salt and his socialistic friends *(Gandhi,* 35), and in 1890 he
joined the London Vegetarian Society (p. 36), many of whose
members, such as Salt and Shaw, were also members of the Fa-
bian Society and the Shelley Society. The philosophical nucleus
of the group that surrounded Salt, according to Ashe, was "the
Simple Life" based on a "highly moral socialism" in which "Love
was to be supreme" (p. 34). "Nonviolence, and nonviolent protest by civil disobedience, were ideas already planted by Shelley
and Thoreau, though civil disobedience remained almost entirely
untried" (p. 34). Ashe considers many of the most important elements of Gandhi's mature philosophy to have been formulated in
his "London phase", and he labels this period in Gandhi's life
"decisive" (p. 40). In the course of his study, Ashe states that
Prometheus Unbound is the "most Gandhian of all long poems"
(p. 212), and he even speculates that Shelley's "The Mask of Anarchy", may have directly given Gandhi the ideas of mass civil disobedience and passive resistance (pp. 103-5).

Although in later life Gandhi on occasion would mention Shelley approvingly, why didn't he specifically credit Shelley's influence on him as he did Thoreau's, Ruskin's, and Tolstoy's? Ashe
suggests that a "Freudian lapse of memory" might have occurred,
"owing to [Gandhi's] disapproval of Shelley's sexual principles"
(p. 105). Ashe has reasonably established that Gandhi in England frequently read about Shelley, and more than likely he often
heard him affectionately spoken about by others, but the specific
nature of Shelley's influence on Gandhi, if any, must, for the
time being at least, remain speculative. My analysis seeks to discuss the similarities that I believe exist between the philosophies
of these two men without attempting to give Shelley particular
credit for influencing Gandhi.

[11] *Gandhi,* 31.

1. HISTORY, NECESSITY, WILL

The concepts of history, necessity, and free will play an important but not always clearly defined role in the philosophies of both Shelley and Gandhi. Recorded history is a circular drama of violence responding to violence from which man must escape. The deterministic lesson that history teaches is the psychologically defeating one that the domination of evil in human affairs is an irreversible fact. Gandhi defines history as "a record of the wars of the world".[12] To continue in Gandhi's words,

Hundreds of nations live in peace. History does not and cannot take note of this fact. History is really a record of every interruption of the even working of the force of love or of the soul. Two brothers quarrel; one of them repents and re-awakens the love that was lying dormant in him; the two again begin to live in peace; nobody takes note of this. But if the two brothers, through the intervention of solicitors or some other reason, take up arms or go to law – which is another form of exhibition of brute force – their doing would be immediately noted in the press, they would be the talk of their neighbors and would probably go down in history. And what is true of families and communities is true of nations. There is no reason to believe that there is one law for families and another for nations. History, then, is a record of an interruption of the course of nature. Soul-force, being natural, is not noted in history.[13]

Shelley's interpretation of history is remarkably similar to Gandhi's. In the words of Professor Duerksen, Shelley interprets history as a persistent "struggle between dictatorship and liberty, in which in general the tendency is toward liberty".[14] Gandhi's "course of nature" is very close to the mature Shelley's concept of Necessity, an amoral force in time with which moral man can align himself through an act of will to escape from the vicious cycles of history. Somewhat paradoxically, man discovers the course of nature, the doctrine of Necessity, through his study of history. Early in his career Shelley had believed in the doctrine of Necessity as it was expounded by William Godwin; the doctrine was one of absolute physical, psychological, and moral

---

[12] *Non-Violent Resistance*, 15.
[13] *Non-Violent Resistance*, 16-17.
[14] *Shelley: Political Writings*, xvii.

determinism.[15] In the "Notes" to *Queen Mab* Shelley states,

Every human being is irresistibly impelled to act precisely as he does act: in the eternity which preceded his birth a chain of causes was generated, which, operating under the name of motives, make it impossible that any thought of his mind, or any action of his life, should be otherwise than it is.[16]

But by the time Shelley wrote *Prometheus Unbound* his view of Necessity had changed. He no longer considered man a slave to Necessity, but a being with free will operating in a universe of Necessarian law. Man's will is free to make a choice between good and evil, and his act of choice will have the inevitable consequences.[17] In such a moral world an act of violence is necessarily self-destructive and an act of forgiveness is necessarily self-liberating. To communicate through word and deed the truth of this moral vision of existence was the goal of both men. Shelley's and Gandhi's belief that their efforts could persuade men to their vision of truth is a testament to their corresponding belief in man's free will. Nonviolence recognizes the law of Necessity; it seeks to counteract the human degradation that inevitably results from violence, and to promote the human liberation that is nonviolence. When all men fully understand the natural law of our existence, a reign of peace will commence. In this sense *Prometheus Unbound* is indeed the "most Gandhian of all long poems".

Man's will and his imagination are not confined by history or by Necessity. Likewise Shelley's "Necessity" and Gandhi's "course of nature" run a course through history independent of the individual human will. Thus Shelley in "A Philosophical View of Reform" states that since certain causes have been set in motion, either reform or civil war is inevitable in England, and Gandhi writes that he sees "coming the day of the rule of the

---

[15] Seymour Reiter, *A Study of Shelley's Poetry* (Albuquerque: University of New Mexico Press, 1967), 51.
[16] *The Complete Works of Percy Bysshe Shelley*, eds. Robert Ingpen and W. E. Peck (New York: Scribner's, 1926-30), I, 144. All further references to Shelley's prose are to this edition and will be given by volume and page within the text. References to his poetry, unless otherwise noted, are also to this edition and will be given by line numbers within the text.
[17] Reiter, 53.

poor, whether that rule be through force of violence or nonviolence".[18] Yet both men clearly realize that if the oppressed attempt to gain liberty through violence they will necessarily continue the historical cycle of revenge and oppression. They realize that the "only real liberation is that which *liberates both the oppressor and the oppressed* at the same time from the same tyrannical automatism of the violent process which contains in itself the curse of irreversibility".[19] Such liberation can come only through nonviolence. The ideal political revolution is a "peaceful transfer of power, effected freely and without compulsion by all concerned, because all have come to recognize it as right".[20] Nonviolence is not a denial of the force of evil in man's world, but a recognition of it and a determination to overcome it through the energy of the human will and the dynamics of Necessity. The individual defines himself and society reforms itself in the nonviolent struggle with evil.

2. LOVE, TRUTH, GOD

In the nonviolent philosophies of Shelley and Gandhi, Truth is God, and Love is God. To quote Gandhi, "*Ahimsa* and Truth are so intertwined that it is practically impossible to disentangle and separate them . . . Nevertheless *ahimsa* is the means; Truth is the end."[21] The means and the end cannot be distinguished in actuality, for Love itself is Truth. God is within man; through nonviolence man expresses the Truth in himself by ceaselessly striving to liberate all men in Truth. Nonviolence presupposes "that human nature in its essence is one and therefore unfailingly responds to the advances to love".[22] Love and Truth are defined only in opposition to hate and untruth.[23] Nonviolence is the perpetual, dynamic struggle of man becoming God through combatting evil

[18]   *Gandhi on Non-Violence,* ed. Thomas Merton (New York: New Directions, 1965), 56.
[19]   Thomas Merton, "Introduction", *Gandhi on Non-Violence*, 14.
[20]   Merton, 23.
[21]   *Non-Violent Resistance*, 42.
[22]   *Gandhi On Non-Violence*, 25.
[23]   *Gandhi On Non-Violence*, 31.

within and without himself. Gandhi at one point defines God as "the living Law of Life . . . the Law and the Lawgiver rolled into one".[24] Shelley once called God "the Soul of the Universe, the spirit of universal imperishable love".[25]

Gandhi says that "Truth is perhaps the most important name of God. In fact it is more correct to say that Truth is God, than to say that God is Truth."[26] The distinction that Gandhi makes is a subtle one, and emphasizes his determination to place God within the human spirit, and not in some inaccessible, superhuman one. Both Shelley and Gandhi emphatically deny the existence of an anthropomorphic god; they deny the existence of the vengeful god of Christianity, as distinguished from what they interpret as the loving God of Jesus Christ. In his "Essay on Christianity" Shelley writes,

The doctrine of what some fanatics have termed a peculiar Providence, that is of some power beyond and superior to that which ordinarily guides the operations of the Universe, interfering to punish the vicious and reward the virtuous – is explicitly denied by Jesus Christ. The absurd and execrable doctrine of vengeance seems to have been contemplated in all its shapes by the great moralist with the profoundest disapprobation. Nor would he permit the most venerable of names to be perverted into a sanction for the meanest and most contemptible propensities incident to the nature of man. "Love your enemies, bless those who curse you that ye may be the sons of your Heavenly Father who makes the sun to shine on the good and the evil, and the rain to fall on the just and the unjust" (VI, 232).

Both Shelley and Gandhi were profoundly influenced by the Sermon on the Mount, and time and again praised it for its spirit of charity, forgiveness, and nonviolence. Both men discovered in the statements of Christ an analogous foundation for their respective religions of love. Shelley writes "that those who are pure in heart shall see God, and that virtue is its own reward, may be considered as equivalent assertions" (VI, 232). Gandhi's response to the teachings of Christ as distinguished from the ethics of Christianity is similar:

[24] *Ibid.*
[25] Letter to Thomas Jefferson Hogg, January 12, 1811 (39).
[26] *Non-Violent Resistance*, 38.

If then, I had to face only the Sermon on the Mount and my own interpretation of it, I should not hesitate to say, "Oh, yes, I am a Christian."
. . . But negatively I can tell you that much of what passes as Christianity is a negation of the Sermon on the Mount. And please mark my
words. I am not at the present moment speaking of the Christian conduct. I am speaking of the Christian belief, of Christianity as it is
understood in the West.[27]

Truth and Love are unchanging absolutes for which man strives
in his continually changing existence on earth. Nonviolence
springs from man's awareness of his spiritual unity with the eternal
verities, and his unified inner vision is manifested by acts of love
in the physical world. Nonviolence is not simply an abstract principle, for, in the words of William Robert Miller, "ultimately
the source of nonviolent power is rooted in love and hinges upon
our ability to express love at a crucial moment in the form of empathy".[28] Empathy on one level is simply seeing things as an opponent sees them, and on a fuller imaginative level it is comprehending an opponent's identity at a given moment in time. The practical results of such empathic love are unselfish acts of charity, tol-
erance, and forgiveness. Shelley writes in "A Defence of Poetry",

The great secret of morals is love; or a going out of our own nature,
and an identification of ourselves with the beautiful which exists in
thought, action, or person, not our own. A man, to be greatly good,
must imagine intensely and comprehensively; he must put himself in
the place of another and many others; the pains and pleasures of his
species must become his own. The great instrument of moral good is
the imagination (VII, 118).

Nonviolence is an inner spiritual experience and an outer physical
experience. It is not a mystical search for perfection, but the discipline of a mind and body committed to realizing Truth on earth.
The first duty of each man is to reform himself so that he will be
able to manifest his inner peace and unity in his efforts to produce
a better society. Reform of self and reform of society are continuous struggles that must go on simultaneously in time. Truth and

[27]   As quoted in Louis Fischer, *The Life of Mahatma Gandhi* (New York:
Collier Books, 1950), 336.
[28]   *Nonviolence: A Christian Interpretation* (New York: Schocken Books,
1966), 159.

Love cannot be captured in a single moment in time and preserved for all eternity; they must be continually recaptured. The non-violent reformer recognizes that the universal elements of Truth, Love, and Peace are within him and that he is within them, and thus his spirit is at perpetual war with the destructive, divisive, and despotic principles fostered by state and church establishments. "When the practice of *ahimsa* becomes universal, God will reign on earth as He does in heaven."[29]

3. REFORM, REVOLUTION, UTOPIA

Ethics and politics are inseparable in Shelley's and Gandhi's visions of life. A political revolution is no revolution at all unless it is accompanied by a moral revolution that liberates the individual's mind from the oppressive hatreds and superstitions of the past. "All reform to be sincere and lasting must come from within."[30] When a so-called political revolution occurs without the attending revolutionary change in the moral vision of the participants, it is simply a changing of roles for the oppressors and the oppressed. There can be no permanent liberation for either party where oppression exists; men remain slaves to their prejudices. Both Shelley and Gandhi prophesied revolutionary goals for society, but their practical contribution to social and political thought is in the revolutionary means that they demanded as a catalyst for reform. And, as has been mentioned before, since the means and ends of nonviolence are themselves inseparable, both Shelley and Gandhi are in a real sense revolutionaries. Neither man expected to see the advent of a Utopian society in his lifetime; both men were committed to gradual reform as the only realistic way to achieve a peaceful society peacefully. The Utopian society of Shelley and Gandhi would be democratic, socialistic, and non-violent.

The first method of reform advocated by these two nonviolent revolutionaries is peaceful persuasion through rational dialogue

---

[29] *Gandhi on Non-Violence*, 25.
[30] Gandhi, *Non-Violent Resistance*, p. 181.

within the constitutional system of the Establishment. If existing conditions within the Establishment make such a method impossible or unfruitful, then the nonviolent militant seeks to create such an atmosphere of confrontation and crisis that dialogue and compromise become the acceptable alternatives to existing injustice for all concerned parties. Common nonviolent means of producing creative energy and tension within the fabric of a society are passive resistance, noncooperation, and civil disobedience. Such tactics are used to "neutralize and ultimately displace violence and enthrone nonviolence in its stead, to replace hatred by love, to replace strife by concord".[31] The creative purpose of such tactics is to turn the life-destroying fury and despair of the oppressed into the life-giving energy and hope of the liberated (pp. 238-39). Where unresponsive tyranny exists civil disobedience is the duty of every citizen. As Gandhi analyzes the problem,

Every State puts down criminal disobedience by force. It perishes, if it does not. But to put down civil disobedience is to attempt to imprison conscience. Civil disobedience can only lead to strength and purity. A civil resister never uses arms and hence he is harmless to a State that is at all willing to listen to the voice of public opinion. He is dangerous for an autocratic State, for he brings about its fall by engaging public opinion upon the matter for which he resists the State. Civil disobedience therefore becomes a sacred duty when the State has become lawless, or which is the same thing, corrupt. And a citizen that barters with such a State shares its corruption or lawlessness. ... It [civil disobedience] is a birthright that cannot be surrendered without surrender of one's self-respect (p. 174).

Acts of passive resistance, non-cooperation, and civil disobedience should be committed selectively in order to be effective and not self-defeating. To quote Gandhi again,

I am resorting to non-co-operation in progressive stages because I want to evolve true order out of untrue order. I am not going to take a single step in non-co-operation unless I am satisfied that the country is ready for that step, namely, non-co-operation will not be followed by anarchy or disorder (p. 160).

Both Shelley and Gandhi considered selective nonviolent tactics against tyranny to operate on at least three intrinsically neces-

[31] *Non-Violent Resistance*, 240.

sary levels. First, a nonviolent campaign, such as mass civil disobedience, fortifies and purifies the spiritual strength and unity of
the individual by testing the quality of love in his soul; second, it
exposes the degree of tyranny present in the opposition and thus
educates society in the true nature of political despotism; and third,
it achieves beneficial, practical results at a specific moment in
time.[32]

Shelley, in "An Address to the Irish People", "A Philosophical
View of Reform", and elsewhere, advises acts of passive resistance, non-cooperation, and civil disobedience as nonviolent methods of securing reform, but he continually emphasizes the need
for selectivity and gradualism in order that the people can comprehend political and social changes as they occur, and thus not
become disorientated, insecure, and fearful – the psychological
conditions conducive to violence. Shelley believed that the French
Revolution failed to accomplish its goals of liberty, equality, and
brotherhood because the people did not truly understand the nonviolent principles upon which these ideals must be founded.

Although Gandhi often disassociated himself from socialistic
and democratic establishments and philosophers, he recognized
the integral part that socialism and democracy would play in a
truly nonviolent society. Gandhi was wary of socialistic and democratic theorizers because they tended to see political change as
an institutional process rather than as the inevitable result of the
will of the people.[33] He also rejected the views of certain philosophers that social evolution was the result of class-war, that the ends
were more important than the means, and that therefore violence
might be justified in such a class-war. However, Gandhi was an
enthusiastic supporter of the "pure" goals of socialism and democracy, and considered them inherently related to nonviolence.

If we wish to evolve the spirit of democracy out of slavery, we must
be scrupulously exact in our dealings with opponents. We may not
replace the slavery of the Government by that of the non-co-opera-
tionists. We must concede to our opponents the freedom we claim
for ourselves and for which we are fighting.[34]

32 Merton, "Introduction", *Gandhi on Non-Violence*, 10.
33 Ashe, *Gandhi*, 249-50.
34 Gandhi, *Non-Violent Resistance*, 147.

Truth and *ahimsa* must incarnate in socialism. In order that they can, the votary must have a living faith in God. Mere mechanical adherence to truth and *ahimsa*, is likely to break down at the critical moment. Hence have I said that truth is God. This God is a living Force. Our life is of that Force. ... The fact is that it has always been a matter of strenuous research to know this great Force and its hidden possibilities. ... This I do say, fearlessly and firmly, that every worthy object can be achieved by the use of Satyagraha. It is the highest and infallible means, the greatest force. Socialism will not be reached by any other means. Satyagraha can rid society of all evils, political, economic and moral.[35]

Shelley also envisions democratic and socialistic principles as ultimate goals in his Utopian society. In "A Philosophical View of Reform" he calls for eventual "universal suffrage", "equal representation" (VII, 47), and states his belief that "equality of possessions must be the last result of the utmost refinements of civilization" (VII, 43). In an "Essay on Christianity" Shelley sympathetically interprets Jesus Christ's particular form of democratic socialism.

Insomuch, therefore, as ye love one another, ye may enjoy the community of whatsoever benefits arise from the inventions of civilized life. ... In proportion to the love existing among men, so will be the community of property and power. Among true and real friends all is common, and were ignorance and envy, and superstition banished from the world all mankind would be as friends. The only perfect and genuine republic is that which comprehends every living being. ... He [Jesus Christ] instructs them that clothing and food and shelter are not, as they suppose, the true end of human life but only certain means to be valued in proportion to their subserviency to that end. These means it is the right of every human being to possess, and that in the same degree. In this respect the fowls of the air and the lilies of the field are examples for the imitation of mankind. They are clothed and fed by the Universal God (VI, 245–48).

In conclusion, it should be emphasized again that both Shelley and Gandhi believed that a nonviolent society is attainable on earth, but that such a society will not be founded on a single heroic act, nor when it is achieved will it be a place of static perfection. A nonviolent society, one such as Shelley envisions at the end of

[35] *Non-Violent Resistance*, 252-53.

Act III of *Prometheus Unbound,* is one of perpetual, creative energy continually renewing its commitment to nonviolence through acts of love. Evil as well as good is eternal; "soul-force" is the ceaseless endeavor to live in Truth through opposition to evil.

III

THE PROSE: "AN ADDRESS TO THE IRISH PEOPLE"

> Let a man overcome anger by love, let him
> overcome evil by good; let him overcome the
> greedy by liberality, the liar by truth!
>
> Budda
>
> I say unto you, That except your righteousness
> shall exceed the righteousness of the scribes and
> Pharisees, ye shall in no case enter into the
> kingdom of heaven.
>
> Matthew 5:20

The perilous political circumstances that existed during Shelley's lifetime enabled the English government to justify the human misery and suffering that it perpetrated on the Irish people. The Irish colony was literally bound in serfdom under the powerful arm of England. The Irish peasant paid tithes to an alien Church, and rent to an alien squirearchy, many of whose members were absentee. In 1792, the year of Shelley's birth, one of the most violent movements to free Ireland from under that oppressive arm was gaining a momentum that frightened concerned Englishmen.[1] England, under Pitt's leadership, considered Wolfe Tone and the United Irishmen movement a threat to England's very existence. The American colonies had successfully declared their free and separate existence, and even more recently, the French people had severed the head of the constitutionally established tyranny of centuries. A world atmosphere charged with revolution had

[1] For general Irish-English historical background during Shelley's lifetime consult: *The Oxford History of England,* ed. G. N. Clark; J. Steven Watson, *The Reign of George III 1760-1815,* vol. XII (Oxford: Clarendon Press, 1960); and E. L. Woodward, *The Age of Reform 1815-1870,* vol. XIII (Oxford: Clarendon Press, 1938).

produced in Irishmen a hopeful frenzy and in Englishmen a dire hysteria. During the years in which the United Irishmen movement was gaining momentum, England was fighting a war with France – a war which the statesmen of England considered to be a precarious do or die situation for their way of life. Ireland's hatred of England's oppression and its religious kinship with Catholic France had fostered much French sympathy in the hearts of Irishmen. Englishmen, on the other hand, realized that if Ireland should be allied to France, England would be hopelessly outflanked. Encouraged by the promise of French assistance, the Irish broke out in open rebellion in 1798. No assistance came, and Castlereagh, Minister for Irish Affairs, under orders from Pitt, brutally and bloodily put down the uprising.

At the turn of the century Pitt turned to diplomatic and political means of controlling the Irish. Although entirely Protestant in membership, the Irish Parliament, the historic achievement of Grattan's leadership, was Ireland's only constitutional institution of protest. This Parliament recently had made prolific use of their rights of free speech and political dissent. Such agitation aroused Pitt, and through wholesale bribery he convinced its members to vote the national institution out of existence, and to merge with the English Parliament in the Act of Union. In exchange for the Act of Union, Pitt promised the Irish to pass a Catholic Emancipation Act. The Act of Union became a fact, Catholic emancipation did not. Pitt discovered that George III refused to sanction Catholic emancipation, and the mentioning of it to him seemed to increase the frequency of his bouts with insanity. Pitt's political power depended upon his alliance with George III, so he promised not to mention Catholic emancipation again, and George tenuously clung to sanity.[2] The Irish, not surprisingly, believed that they had been sold down the river.

In 1810, just before Shelley's arrival in Dublin, the first great Irish national movement of the nineteenth century had begun under the leadership of Daniel O'Connell. The Catholic Committee's

[2] As G. M. Trevelyan states: "The age of chivalry was not dead" (*British History in the Nineteenth Century and After* [1937; rpt. New York: Harper & Row, 1966], 104).

avowed political purposes were two: Catholic emancipation and repeal of the Act of Union.

Into this violent, exciting, chaotic world stepped Percy Bysshe Shelley, a youth of nineteen.[3] On the night of February 12, 1812, after a turbulent voyage, Shelley, his wife Harriet, and her sister Eliza arrived in Dublin, a troubled city of about 200,000 residents.[4] The magnanimous if somewhat naive purpose of Shelley's journey was to liberate the Irish, or rather to inspire the Irish to liberate themselves from the political and economic tyranny of England and the intellectually stultifying oppression of Catholicism. Ireland had been selected by the enthusiastic young radical to be the beginning of a world-wide movement of social and economic reform.[5] Ireland, somewhat predictably, declined the honor. But Shelley's experiences in Ireland, and the pamphlets which he penned at this time, are important to the growth of the man and his work. This chapter will concentrate on discovering Shelley's thought in the pamphlet "An Address to the Irish People" which he wrote in Keswick before embarking for Ireland. Specific notice will be taken of the nonviolent approach that Shelley recommends to bring about social reform.

1

In his "Address" Shelley warns the Irish: "Never do evil that good may come" (V, 225).[6] We may perhaps paraphrase the Tory government's official position in regard to Ireland as: Never do good that evil may come. Certainly the revolutionaries in France

---

[3] The most helpful critical studies on Shelley's life and works during this period are Carl Grabo, *The Magic Plant*, 37-119; Newman Ivey White, *Shelley I*, 203-28; Kenneth Neill Cameron, *The Young Shelley*, 128-58; and John Pollard Guinn, *Shelley's Political Thought*, 11-45.

[4] White, *Shelley* I, 203.

[5] On January 29, 1812, Shelley wrote to Elizabeth Hitchner: "Come, come to Ireland ... Come, come, and share with us the noblest success or the most glorious martyrdom" (164).

[6] This maxim, slightly restated, appears again on the broadside Shelley wrote in Dublin to be posted about the town. Article XVII of "A Declaration of Rights" reads: "No man has a right to do an evil thing that good may come" (V, 273).

thought that they had been doing good, but look at the evil that resulted. Therefore, the Tory governments of Spencer Perceval and Lord Liverpool were dedicated to preserving the status quo in Ireland during the ten years 1810-20. They were terrified at the power of Napoleon and the threat of invasion, and they were petrified at the permeation of egalitarian doctrines which threatened their plush aristocratic way of life. Since change, even for the good, meant an egalitarian compromise and a lessening of their power and wealth, they steadfastly opposed all change. Shelley realized that the preservation of the status quo was a myth – that change was inevitable. Thus he hated the defenders of the Establishment as tyrants and despots, and believed that in reality they were protecting their own lucrative position and oppressing the majority of mankind.

In "An Address to the Irish People", as in all his political writings, Shelley's altruistic purpose was to educate men's minds and awaken their imaginations to the forces of change, so that an educated society would be better able to assimilate change through nonviolent means and make it work for the happiness and fulfillment of all men.[7] Specifically, Shelley agitates for two practical reforms: the repeal of the Act of Union and Catholic emancipation.[8] It is significant that neither of these proposals requests a blind step forward into the unknown future (unknown in a political sense), but rather both desire a return to the previous political freedom and independence that the Irish had once known. Yet

[7] Roland A. Duerksen points out: "In poetry as well as prose he [Shelley] sought to point out that the way to a better life for all mankind, especially for the unfortunate masses, is to change man's thinking rather than to enforce revolutions by political and military means" (*Shelleyan Ideas in Victorian Literature,* 15).

[8] For an unsympathetic view of Shelley's Irish writings, see A. M. D. Hughes, *The Nascent Mind of Shelley* (Oxford: Clarendon Press, 1947). "Repetitious, badly arranged, with some fustian in places, the Irish writings have also the lipidity and onflow of Shelley's style and a high-mindedness not without charm. But they are the work of one ignorant of the situation. The *Address* especially is behind the times or wide of them altogether" (p. 131). For an enthusiastic appreciation of Shelley's Irish writings, see Cameron, *The Young Shelley.* "The outstanding value of the *Address* lies in its sense of historical evolution and its insistence on transcending a narrow middleclass outlook" (p. 139).

this pose was simply a matter of strategy on Shelley's part; he did not desire a return to the past tyrannies of Irish history. Instead, he was looking forward to the repeal of these two acts as a beginning of a new age in history, an age marked by universal emancipation, philanthropy, enlightened citizenry,[9] equality under the law, and a just and reasonable distribution of wealth.[10]

Shelley emphasizes that the immediate changes he recommends for Ireland are wholly within the English constitutional system, and that they should be enacted by traditionally constitutional means – that is, through legislation in the English Parliament. He does not recommend open rebellion or a movement for Irish independence, for such changes would be too swift and radical, producing more harm than good. Nor is he deceived by what the immediate results of Catholic emancipation and the repeal of the Union Act would be. They would not be a cure-all; indeed, they would cure very little. But such reforms would be a beginning.[11]

Although we may see many things put in train, during our life-time, we cannot hope to see the work of virtue and reason finished now; we can only lay the foundation for our posterity. ... I look upon Catholic Emancipation, and the restoration of the liberties and happiness of Ireland, so far as they are compatible with the English Constitution, as great and important events. I hope to see them soon. But if all ended here, it would give me little pleasure – I should still see thousands miserable and wicked, things would still be wrong....

---

[9] To Elizabeth Hitchner (January 26) Shelley writes that the "Address" "is intended to familiarize to uneducated apprehensions ideas of liberty, benevolence, *peace* and toleration. It is *secretly* intended also as a preliminary to other pamphlets to shake Catholicism at its basis, and to induce Quakerish and Socinian principle[s] of politics, without objecting to the Christian Religion, which would do no good to the vulgar just now, and cast an odium over the principles which are advanced" (162). The italics are Shelley's.

[10] "A Philosophical View of Reform" is the most concise statement of Shelley's socialistic principles. "Equality in possessions must be the last result of the utmost refinements of civilization; it is one of the conditions of that system of society, towards which with whatever hope of ultimate success, it is our duty to tend." (VII, 43).

[11] Floyd Stovall comments: "His [Shelley's] desire for the immediate accomplishment of his ideal was satisfied in poetry, where he could overleap all restraints; but in prose he attempted to adjust himself to actual conditions and to adopt the practical methods of other reformers" (*Desire and Restraint in Shelley* [Durham: Duke University Press, 1932], 132).

But I cannot expect a rapid change. Many are obstinate and determined in their vice, whose selfishness makes them think only of their
own good, when in fact, the best way even to bring that about, is to
make others happy. I do not wish to see things changed now, because
it cannot be done without violence (V, 232-33).

Combining the eighteenth century's confidence in reason with the
nineteenth century's faith in progress, Shelley believed that change
in man's social condition was inevitable, and that this change
must be gradual in order to be accepted peacefully. He believed
with other pre-Darwin thinkers, such as Emerson and Tennyson,
that this change would coincide with man's ethical evolution up-
ward.[12] As man became better his society would become better,
and Shelley had the Romantic faith that such was possible, and
even probable. It was the principal motivation behind his writing
of the "Address".

The crisis to which I allude as the period of your emancipation, is not
the death of the present king, or any circumstance that has to do
with kings, but something that is much more likely to do you good:
it is the increase of virtue and wisdom which will lead people to find
out that force and oppression are wrong and false; and this opinion,
when it once gains ground, will prevent government from severity.
It will restore those rights which government has taken away. Have
nothing to do with force or violence, and things will safely and surely
make their way to the right point (V, 228).

Twenty-six years later, in 1838, Ralph Waldo Emerson in his essay "On War" could add an articulate theory to Shelley's idealistic hope.

And so it is not a great matter how long men refuse to believe the
advent of peace: war is on its last legs; and a universal peace is as
sure as is the prevalence of civilization over barbarism, of liberal
governments over feudal forms. The question for us is only *How*
soon? . . . War and peace thus resolve themselves into a mercury of
the state of cultivation. At a certain stage of his progress, the man
fights, if he be of a sound body and mind. At a certain higher stage,

---

[12]   Shelley had read Erasmus Darwin whose works were in the library at
Field Place. Grabo, 4 and 66. Also see Desmond King-Hele, "The Influence
of Erasmus Darwin on Shelley", *Keats-Shelley Memorial Bulletin*, XIII
(1962), 30-36; and "Erasmus Darwin's Influence on Shelley's Early Poems",
Keats-Shelley Memorial Bulletin, XVI (1965), 26-8.

he makes no offensive demonstration, but is alert to repel injury, and of an unconquerable heart. At a still higher stage, he comes into the region of holiness; passion has passed away from him; his war-like nature is all converted into an active medicinal principle; he sacrifices himself, and accepts with alacrity wearisome tasks of denial and charity; but, being attacked, he bears it and turns the other cheek, as one engaged, throughout his being, no longer to the service of an individual but to the common soul of all men.[13]

Emerson's "region of holiness" was the aspiration of Shelley. "When one cheek is struck, turn the other to the insulting coward" (V, 238). But as we shall see, there is a distinct difference between each man's approach to Utopia. Shelley's commitment to civilization was a passionate one. Thus while Emerson separates passion from holiness, Shelley not only integrates passion as an active principle in man's search for peace, but views passionate commitment to nonviolent reform as a holy act.

Shelley's and Emerson's faith in man's potential for good combined with their apparent sophistical reasoning, often leads twentieth century man to turn away from the Romantic promise.[14] But the problem of human violence still remains, and today the advent of sophisticated, nuclear warfare threatens man's very existence. In our century, the promise of the Romantic vision has again been held out to us through men such as Mohandas Gandhi and Martin Luther King – men who saw a discrepancy between man's reality and his potential, and who attempted to do something to bring man closer to his potential, spiritually and realistically. Such a man also was Shelley, and his "Address" which contains the basic principles of his political thought has been too easily dismissed by scholars today, as it was by readers in Shelley's time.[15] The nonviolent strategy for social reform which he offers

13 *Emerson's Complete Works* (Boston: Houghton, Mifflin, and Company, 1886), XI, 188-9; 193-4.
14 Emerson's argument, although modified, is still viable in the twentieth century. "Meanwhile we may rest on the assurance that whatever makes for cultural development is working also against war" (Sigmund Freud, "Letter to Albert Einstein: Why War?" in *The Pacifist Conscience*, ed. Peter Mayer [Chicago: Henry Ridgeway Company, 1967], 248).
15 One scholar who does recognize the significance of the "Address" to Shelley's thought is Carl Grabo. "If the *Address* and Shelley's purpose in it are absurd, then Shelley is absurd, and readers of him should content

as an alternative to violence is still viable today. We must remember that if we judge Shelley, Gandhi, and King as political failures, then we are judging the men and the circumstances, and not necessarily the truth that guided them.[16]

2

Shelley begins "An Address to the Irish People" by giving a brief historical survey of violence, specifically connecting violence with organized religion, and then making a call for universal brotherhood not bound by the limitations of religion and nationality. All men must recognize the "spirit of universal harmony" (V, 217), Shelley's concept of God, that binds them together. Shelley's historical sketch of the violent and divisive qualities of organized religion commences with an omission that is of interest to us in our study.

No one knows much of the early times of the Christian religion, until about three-hundred years after its beginning, two great churches, called the Roman and the Greek Churches, divided the opinions of men. They fought for a very long time, a great many words were wasted and a great deal of blood shed (V, 217).

The early times of the Christian religion are known, and if Shelley had been aware of the pre-Constantine history of the Church, he would have found excellent material to defend his proposals for nonviolent resistance.[17] For the members of the early Church

---

themselves with the melody of his lines and the colorful pictures of aerial phenomena which are characteristic of his verse. Shelley was deadly serious in his efforts to win the Irish people to the spirit of reform. The ideas which he expounds he had made his own by his passionate belief in them. They are ideas which were never held by more than a minority at any time and are scarcely more popular now than in Shelley's day" (The Magic Plant, 67).
[16] Gandhi's belief was that "Ahimsa is always infallible. When, therefore, it appears to have failed, the failure is due to the inaptitude of the votary." Or again: "There is no such thing as defeat in non-violence" (Gandhi on Non-Violence, 75 and 24).
[17] For an extensive analysis of early Christian attitudes toward war and violence, see Cecil John Cadoux, The Early Christian Attitude Toward War (London: Headley Brothers, 1919).

resisted nonviolently the tyrannies of the pagan emperors. There is good evidence that one of the accepted doctrines of early Christianity was pacifism.[18] But Shelley goes on to show how organized religions, both Catholic and Protestant, have divided and subdued their subjects by fear and violence.

Doubt everything that leads you not to charity, and think of the word "heretic" as a word which some selfish knave invented for the ruin and misery of the world, to answer his own paltry and narrow ambition. Do not inquire if a man be a heretic, if he be a Quaker, or a Jew, or a Heathen; but if he be a virtuous man, if he loves liberty and truth, if he wishes the happiness and peace of human kind (V, 219-20).

According to Shelley, the orthodox churches have consistently acted as if might makes right and as if belief can be forced on an individual. He declares both strategies wrong, morally and realistically, because "force makes the side that employs it directly wrong" (V, 233), and because "we cannot believe just what we like, but only what we think to be true" (V, 221). The mission of the nonviolent reformer is to destroy the superstitions that divide and promulgate the truths that unite.

From what has been said I think we may be justified in concluding, that people of all religions ought to have an equal share in the state, that the words heretic and orthodox were invented by a vain villain, and have done a great deal of harm in the world, and that no person is answerable for his belief whose actions are virtuous and moral, that the religion is best whose members are the best men, and that no person can help either his belief or disbelief. – Be in charity with all men (V, 222).

But how is one to operate in a potentially violent situation without contributing to the bloodshed? There are many strategies available to the reformer once he accepts the principle of nonviolence.

... We now come to the method of doing these things. I agree with the Quakers so far as they disclaim violence, and trust their cause wholly and solely to its own truth. – If you are convinced of the truth of your cause, trust wholly to its truth; if you are not convinced,

---

[18] For example, "The Trial of Maximilianus", in *The Quiet Battle*, ed. Mulford Q. Sibley (Boston: Beacon Press, 1963), 17.

give it up. In no case employ violence; the way to liberty and happiness is never to transgress the rules of virtue and justice. Liberty and happiness are founded upon virtue and justice, if you destroy the one, you destroy the other (V, 224).

To employ violence, even in a just cause, is self-defeating.

I will fondly hope that the schemes for your happiness and liberty, as well as those for the happiness and liberty of the world, will not be wholly fruitless. One secure method of defeating them is violence on the side of the injured party. If you can descend to use the same weapons as your enemy, you put yourself on a level with him on this score, you must be convinced that he is on these grounds your superior. But appeal to the sacred principles of virtue and justice, then how is he awed into nothing? How does truth show him in his real colours, and place the cause of toleration and reform in the clearest light? (V, 224).

Realistically, the Irish cannot hope to defeat the British in a violent conflict. But just as realistically, the Irish can hope to defeat the British in a nonviolent conflict. For in a nonviolent conflict moral not military superiority is necessary for victory. Truth and justice align with the party that desires love and brotherhood, thus giving it the moral power to erase hatred and oppression. In 1812, popular support in England to British suppression of the Irish was founded on the assumption that the British were morally superior to the rowdy, drunken papists.[19] Should this stereotype be destroyed, or perhaps even reversed, popular support of Britain's Irish policies would disappear at home and abroad. Thus to be victorious the Irish must refrain from all violence in order to deny the British an excuse to justify their atrocities.[20] "Be warm in your cause, yet rational, and charitable, and tolerant – never let the oppressor grind you into justifying his conduct by imitating his meanness" (V, 226).

[19] Shelley's understanding that moral superiority is necessary before victory can come through nonviolence makes him feel obligated to divorce the Irish from what he considers to be the immoralities of Catholicism ("Nothing on earth is infallible. The Priests that pretend to it, are wicked and mischievous imposters ...." V, 242), and the immoralities of their social customs ("Lay up money with which you usually purchase drunkenness and ill-health, to relieve the pains of your fellow-sufferers" V, 226).

[20] A classic essay on strategy in a nonviolent conflict, such as Shelley proposes, is Richard B. Gregg's, "Moral Jiu-Jitsu", in *The Power of Non-*

For both ethical and pragmatic reasons, Shelley urges the Irish to agitate for social reform through nonviolent means. To willfully commit violence in the interest of social reform is wrong. One must "Never do evil that good may come", – sacred goals demand sacred means. We live the means, not the goals. Shelley recognizes that his sacred goals of universal justice, love, and respect for truth – the basis of his Utopian nonviolent society – could only be realized when the citizenry understood the twin philosophical truths that nonviolence is the way to peace and brotherhood, and that violence accomplishes nothing permanent; it only continues the destructive impulse in human behavior that forfeits the ability to create liberty and equality. Nothing is "so well fitted to produce slavery, tyranny, and vice as the violence which is attributed to the friends of liberty, and which the real friends of liberty are the only persons who disdain" (V, 234). In the "Address" Shelley is at pains to separate in the public mind righteousness and truth from force and violence.

An Act passed in the British Parliament to take away the rights of Catholics to act in that assembly, does not really take them away. It prevents them from doing it by force. This is in such cases, the last and only efficacious way. But force is not the test of truth; they will never have recourse to violence who acknowledge no other rule of behavior but virtue and justice (V, 221).

In addition to the obvious fact that England's potential in terms of arms and manpower is much greater than Ireland's, Shelley gives several other practical reasons why the Irish should shun violence in attempting to further their cause. To use violence would give the enemy a satisfying justification for crushing any movement for reform, and thus painfully delaying it. It would take the movement out of the hands of the people, and would

---

violence (New York: Schocken Books, 1959), 43-52. This essay is perhaps the best known statement on the tactical strategy of nonviolence now in print, and Shelley in his "Address" anticipates much of its content. Gregg asserts that the focus of the conflict arises from the interaction between nonviolence, truth, and self. "The art of jiu-jitsu is based on a knowledge of balance and how to disturb it. In a struggle of moral jiu-jitsu, the retention of moral balance seems to depend upon the qualities of one's relationship to moral truth. Hence part of the superior power of the nonviolent resister seems to lie in the nature of his character" (46).

create an atmosphere that would see new oppressors take the place of the old – as in France. Shelley leaves little doubt that he believes that in Ireland these new oppressors would come from the ranks of bishops and priests in the Church establishment.[21] Shelley realized through Godwin[22] that revolutionary upheavals usually created more oppression than existed previously. When violence erupts the entire community becomes polarized and forced to seek protection in separate camps. The atmosphere is charged with fear, deceit, censorship; the main artillery for the pursuit of truth, the free and open examination and discussion of experience and ideas, is shattered. Such a situation portends despotism. But perhaps violence is seen as most futile when judged by its success in accomplishing its acknowledged goals. It never solves a problem – it only temporarily eliminates indications of it. Violence is fruitless because it cannot change the human mind: "you cannot alter a man's opinion by beating and burning, but by persuading him that what you think is right, and this can only be done by fair words and reason" (V, 221). Violence cannot effect a lasting change; nonviolence with its appeal to the reason and imagination can effect meaningful change. The change will be meaningful because the leaders and citizenry understand the purpose of reform and accept it willingly, as opposed to change enforced by fear of punishment and thus resented by the populace.

One must act in two ways in a nonviolent campaign: education of self, and strategic group-action. Shelley reiterates throughout his writings in poetry and prose that revolution begins with the individual. "Before Government is done away with, we must reform ourselves" (V, 232). "It [Utopian change] is founded on the

---

[21] "They [potential new oppressors] will, I doubt not, attempt to rescue you from your present miserable state, but they will prepare a worse. It will be out of the frying-pan into the fire. Your present oppressors, it is true, will then oppress you no longer, but you will feel the lash of a master a thousand times more blood-thirsty and cruel. Evil designing men will spring up who will prevent your thinking as you please, will burn you if you do not think as they do. There are always bad men who take advantage of hard times. The monks and priests of old were very bad men; take care no such abuse your confidence again" (V, 219).

[22] See "On Revolutions", in Enquiry Concerning Political Justice, ed. F. E. L. Priestly (Toronto: University of Toronto Press, 1946), I, 263-84.

reform of private men, and without individual amendment it is vain and foolish to expect the amendment of a state or government" (V, 236). This reform of self is to be both moral and educational. Reading, discussing, and listening rather than drinking, carousing, and arguing are to fill one's spare time. Men should gather together in an attempt to discover the truth about the relevant issues of their existence, and to plan nonviolent strategies for reform. War and poverty are the relevant issues of the age, and Shelley gives the Irish immediate nonviolent strategies to be employed, and he proposes an "organization of a society, whose institution shall serve as a bond to its members, for the purposes of virtue, happiness, liberty, and wisdom, by the means of intellectual opposition to grievances" (V, 245).

The first step in preparing for a nonviolent campaign directed at improving some unjust social condition is education. Each person must educate himself and his family in political and social action and develop an awareness of the eternal law of change, so that change does not produce violence, suffering, and despair, but rather peaceful acceptance and human development.[23]

Think, read, and talk; let your own condition and that of your wives and children, fill your minds; disclaim all manner of alliance with violence; meet together if you will, but do not meet in a mob. If you think and read and talk with a real wish of benefiting the cause of truth and liberty, it will soon be seen how true a service you are rendering, and how sincere you are in your professions; but mobs and violence must be discarded (V, 229).

The chief benefit of such education is that it does away with the conditions that foster oppression; it eliminates fear and supersti-

[23] Because of the ignorance of the common people, Shelley admitted he was against immediate universal suffrage. "With respect to Universal Suffrage, I confess I consider its adoption, in the present unprepared state of public knowledge and feeling, a measure fraught with peril .... The consequences of the immediate extension of the elective franchise to every male adult, would be to place power in the hands of men who have been rendered brutal and torpid and ferocious by ages of slavery" ("A Proposal for Putting Reform to the Vote Throughout the Kingdom", VI, 68). "Mr. Bentham and other writers have urged the admission of females to the right of suffrage; this attempt seems somewhat immature" ("A Philosophical View of Reform", VII, 44).

tion that hinder social progress, and as men emerge from the depths of ignorance they acquire the knowledge to effect meaningful reform.[24] To Shelley, the pursuit of truth was synonymous with the attempt to understand and benefit the human condition. At this particular time and circumstance, "the only subjects" for thought, study, and discussion "are those of happiness and liberty" (V, 224). Shelley gives a specific example of a topic that should be considered.

You have much to think of. – Is war necessary to your happiness and safety? The interest of the poor gains nothing from wealth and extension of a nation's boundaries, they gain nothing from glory, a word that has often served as a cloak to the ambition or avarice of Statesmen. ... The poor purchase this glory and this wealth, at the expense of their blood and labor, and happiness, and virtue. They die in battle for this infernal cause. Their labor supplies money and food for carrying it into effect; their happiness is destroyed by the oppression they undergo, their virtue is rooted out by the depravity and vice that prevail throughout the army, and which under the present system, is perfectly unavoidable (V, 238-9).

Obviously Shelley is not only urging the Irish to think. But his anti-war stand is consistent with the principal focus of his nonviolent position. The oppressed in their battle for freedom and justice should not stoop to the violent tactics of their oppressors; neither should they be accomplices or agents in that violence which is the real power of the oppressors. The Irish should refuse to serve in war not only for moral reasons,[25] but because in a strictly utilitarian sense they will derive no benefit and incur many hardships. Military power is the chief weapon of a despot, and the common people by participating in the military – by wearing

[24] Elsewhere, Shelley argues similarly from a different perspective. He asserts that it is in the interest of the educated and wealthy to educate and relieve the suffering masses; otherwise there is "a ready field for any adventurer who should wish for whatever purpose to incite a few ignorant men to acts of illegal outrage" ("An Address to the People on the Death of Princess Charlotte", VI, 79).
[25] In "A Declaration of Rights", composed in Dublin in 1812, Shelley states: "Man has no right to kill his brother, it is no excuse that he does so in uniform. He only adds the infamy of servitude to the crime of murder" (V, 273).

a uniform, by paying taxes, by quartering soldiers – give the strength to the arm that beats them.[26]

Secrecy, another practice of oppressors and false-prophets, is to be abhorred by all men sincerely interested in truth and justice.

Associations for purposes of violence are entitled to the strongest disapprobation of the real reformist. Always suspect that some knavish rascal is at the bottom of things of this kind, waiting to profit by the confusion. All secret associations are also bad. Are you men of deep designs, whose deeds love darkness better than light; dare you not say what you think before any man, can you not meet in the open face of day in conscious innocence? Oh, Irishmen ye can! Hidden arms, secret meetings and designs, violently to separate England from Ireland, are all very bad. I do not mean to say the very end of them is bad, the object you have in view may be just enough, while the way you go about it is wrong, may be calculated to produce an opposite effect (V, 225).

As it was to Godwin, secrecy was repugnant to Shelley.[27] His life-long hatred of secrecy for both ethical and practical reasons is similar to Gandhi's:

No secret organization, however big, could do any good. Secrecy aims at building a wall of protection around you. *Ahimsa* disdains all such protection. It functions in the open in the face of odds, the heaviest conceivable. We have to organize for action a vast people that have been crushed under the heel of unspeakable tyranny for centuries. They cannot be organized by other than open, truthful means. I have

---

[26] Compare Leo Tolstoy: "The government, and all those people of the upper classes that are near the government, and that live by the work of others, need some means of dominating the workers, and this means they find in their control of the army.... They provoke their own people and some foreign government, and then pretend that for the well-being or for the defence of their people they must declare war, which again brings profit only to generals, officers, functionaries, merchants, and, in general, to the rich. In reality war is an inevitable result of the existence of armies; and armies are only needed by governments in order to dominate their own working classes" ("Letter to a Non-commissioned Officer", in *The Pacifist Conscience*, 161).

[27] Shelley consistently argued against secret associations and the principle of secrecy in general. He even took a firm stand against the secret ballot, declaring that a vote motivated by truth and justice should be cast in an open and honorable manner. "A Philosophical View of Reform", VII, 44. For the view of a commentator who believes that Shelley compromised his stand against secrecy, see Gerald McNiece, 106-8.

grown up from youth to seventy-six years in abhorrence of secrecy. There must be no watering down of the ideal.[28]

Both Shelley and Gandhi were driven by unique visions of what society could be, and in the pursuit of that attainment they recommended only those means that would exist in the ideal nonviolent state. Thus Shelley in the "Address" recommends for individual and collective action education through thinking, reading, and discussing, openness and honesty, brotherhood and philanthropy, work and abstinence,[29] discipline and unity,[30] and forgiveness of sins.[31] Each recommendation is also fundamental to Gandhi's philosophy of nonviolence.

3

Shelley's advice to the Irish people is not simply intended as a guide to the contemplative life of "socially involved" people. It is a call to action. It is a call for nonviolent resistance and civil disobedience.[32] This aspect of the "Address" has been frequently overlooked by Shelley scholars, who have been too quick to take Shelley's assurance to his apprehensive friends, Elizabeth Hitchner and William Godwin, that he was doing nothing to get him into trouble with the government.[33] But in proposing that men meet

---

[28] *Gandhi on Non-Violence*, 40.
[29] "And I have opened to your view a new scene – does not your heart bound at the bare possibility of your posterity possessing that liberty and happiness of which during our lives powerful exertions and habitual abstinence may give us a foretaste?" (V, 243).
[30] "And never quarrel between each other, be all of one mind as nearly as you can; do these things, and I will promise you liberty and happiness" (V, 230).
[31] "I earnestly desire peace and harmony: – peace, that whatever wrongs you may have suffered, benevolence and a spirit of forgiveness should mark your conduct towards those who have persecuted you" (V, 241).
[32] It is at this point that Shelley significantly differs from William Godwin and his philosophy presented in *Political Justice*. Godwin consistently disengaged himself from Shelley's political activism, and specifically Shelley's intention of arousing the Irish to active resistance.
[33] White, 210. Roland Duerksen is one scholar who recognizes the "assertive or activistic emphasis" of Shelley's Irish writings (*Shelley's Political Writings*, xi).

together to discuss social injustice and political reform, Shelley was advising the Irish to nonviolently defy the law.[34] Any such gathering of men would have been declared illegal under a series of Seditious Practices and Assemblies Acts,[35] which prohibited any meetings for the purpose of discussing reforms in Church and State. Shelley was well aware that he was recommending civil disobedience to an unjust law.

Government will not allow a peaceable and reasonable discussion of its principles by any association of men, who assemble for that express purpose. But have not human beings a right to assemble to talk upon what subject they please? ... Although I deprecate violence, and the cause which depends for its influence on force, yet I can by no means think that assembling together merely to talk of how things go on, I can by no means think that societies formed for talking on any subject however government may dislike them, come in any way under the head of force or violence. ... Are you slaves, or are you men? If slaves, then crouch to the rod, and lick the feet of your oppressors; glory [in] your shame, it will become you if brutes to act according to your nature. But you are men, a real man is free, so far as circumstances will permit him. Then firmly, yet quietly resist. ... Let the object of your associations (for I conceal not my approval of assemblies conducted with regularity, *peaceableness* and thought for any purpose), be the amendment of these abuses (V, 238–40; italics Shelley's).

Shelley's "Proposals for an Association of Philanthropists" was an even more direct call for action. "An Address to the Irish People" was written for the average, little-educated Irishman who had no training in political philosophy. Shelley's "Proposals" was written to the erudite minority, and propounds the same reforms as the earlier pamphlet, as well as proposing an association

[34] In "A Philosophical View of Reform" Shelley advises similar measures for the British people: "The public opinion in England ought first to [be] excited to action, and the durability of those forms within which the oppressors intrench themselves brought perpetually to the test of its operation. No law or institution can last if this opinion be distinctly pronounced against it. For this purpose government ought to be defied, in cases of questionable result, to prosecute for political libel. All questions relating to the jurisdiction of magistrates and courts of law respecting which any doubt could be raised ought to be agitated with indefatigable pertinacity" (VII, 51).

[35] Goldwin Smith, *A History of England* (New York: Scribner, 1966), pp. 523-24. "In 1795 the passage of the Treasonable and Seditious Practices Act and the Seditious Assemblies Act gave further evidence of the panic caused

of educated and well-meaning men to organize for the purpose of ideological exchange and the education of the uneducated majority. Besides its avowed purposes of Catholic emancipation, repeal of the Act of Union, and the Association, the "Proposals" discusses many of the themes found in the "Address": the rights of free speech, press, and assembly,[36] social philanthropy, nonviolence, the need for gradual as opposed to rapid change, and the need for an educated public.

What is of specific interest to us is Shelley's strategy in recommending, generally in the "Address" and specifically in the "Proposals", such an illegal association. The unique concept in terms of nonviolent strategy is that Shelley proposes openly breaking the law. He proposes an association he knows to be illegal, and then demands that it not be a secret organization – that all the proceedings of the association be open – that its members in protest of an unjust law be ready to accept any punishment and persecution that might result.

I propose, then, to such as think with me a Philanthropic Association, in spite of the danger that may attend the attempt. I do not this beneath the shroud of mystery and darkness. I propose not an Association of Secrecy. Let it be open as the beam of day. Let it rival the sunbeam in its stainless purity, as in the extensiveness of its effulgence.

I disclaim all connection with insincerity and concealment. The latter implies the former, as much as the former stands in the need of the latter. It is a very latitudinarian system of morality that permits its professor to employ bad means for any end whatever.

---

by events across the Channel. There was now no chance to agitate for reform. So far as the government was concerned reform meant the same thing as revolution. This harsh series of repressive acts took away from a large part of the population its only way of expressing an opinion; because it was not represented in Parliament it could say nothing without being liable to punishment under the new mussling legislation." For a discussion of the specific provisions of these Acts and the circumstances that made them law, see W. L. Laprade, *England and the French Revolution, 1789-1797* in *Johns Hopkins University Studies*, XXVII (Baltimore, 1909), 585-88.
[36] "A Letter to Lord Ellenborough", written shortly after Shelley's return from Ireland, is an eloquent defense of man's basic freedoms (V, 253-70). Cameron states that this essay "is Shelley's first important work of literature, a work to be ranked among the classics of the struggle for freedom of speech" (*The Young Shelley*, 186).

Weapons which vice *can* use are unfit for the hand of virtue. Concealment implies falsehood; it is bad, and can therefore never be serviceable to the cause of philanthropy (V, 259).

Such strategy was likewise fundamental to the nonviolent campaigns of Mohandas K. Gandhi and Martin Luther King. Shelley's strategy can be reduced even further and examined in the light of twentieth century nonviolent thought. Like Shelley, both Gandhi and King took upon themselves the enormous task of freeing people from the bondage in which they had been placed through social and political discrimination. Each man in the pursuit of social justice through nonviolent means used civil disobedience as a tactic. But in each campaign they selected one specific issue on which to focus their demands for total justice – Gandhi such laws as the Black Act in South Africa and the Salt Acts in India, and King such laws as the segregation statutes of the American South. Although Shelley dreams of complete social equality for all men, he realizes that change must be gradual, and therefore rather than urging mass non-cooperation or civil disobedience to all unjust laws, he selects one on which the Irish people should focus. His selection was prudent, and indeed necessary for a successful campaign. Shelley's entire program for reform hinged on the free and open discussion of ideas. In the "Address" he decries all laws that prohibit or limit freedom of speech, press, or assembly. These freedoms are essential for man in his pursuit of truth and his attempts to secure freedom and justice. They cannot be denied. So Shelley recommends open disobedience of the Seditious Assemblies Act if the Irish are "men" and not "slaves". Such a move would provide a focus for the badly divided Irish to unite themselves, and reestablish a sense of dignity – dignity not only as Irishmen, but as human beings.

4

Before we conclude this chapter we should be aware of the ethical dilemma that confronted Shelley in his Irish venture, a dilemma that has since confronted other nonviolent reformers.

Simply stated, the problem results from the reformer's realization that his proposals given in the spirit of nonviolence may indeed produce violence when acted upon by the untrained, the uneducated, and the oppressed. Godwin opposed Shelley's Irish venture from the start because he feared the violence that might result, and the consequent setback which violence would give to the movement for reform. In his letter of March 4, Godwin writes Shelley that "your views and mine as to improvement of mankind are decisively at issue".

If I may be allowed to understand my book on *Political Justice,* its pervading principle is that association is a most ill-chosen and ill-qualified mode of endeavoring to promote the political happiness of mankind. And I think of your pamphlet, however commendable and lovely are many of the sentiments it contains, that it will be either ineffective to its immediate object, or that it has no very remote tendency to light again the flames of rebellion and war. ... You may as well tell the adder not to sting ... as tell organized societies of men, associated to obtain their rights and to extinguish opposition, prompted by a deep aversion to inequality, luxury, enormous taxes and the evils of war, to be innocent, to employ no violence, and calmly to await the progress of truth.[37]

In his reply Shelley rejects Godwin's advice concerning refraining from active participation in the movement for reform. He writes that his Irish pamphlets were not to be a restatement of *Political Justice,* but an extension to it – a tactic for a changing world. After all, "*Political Justice* was first published in 1793, nearly twenty years have elapsed since the general direction of its doctrines. What has followed? have men ceased to fight, has vice and misery vanished from the earth?" (173). No, reform cannot be relegated to a parlor-room discussion by the educated minority; that is why "the *Address* was principally designed to operate on the Irish *mob*" (173). Yet Shelley proposes to the Irish "No violent or immediate measures", and therefore he does not think that his writings "can in the slightest degree tend to violence".

The pains which I have taken even to tautology to insist on pacific measures, the necessity which every warrior and rebel must lay under

[37] Thomas Jefferson Hogg, *The Life of Percy Bysshe Shelley* (London: Routledge and Sons, 1906), 322-3.

to deny almost every passage of my book before he can become so, must at least exculpate *me* from tending to make him so (173).

Action, as well as contemplation and discussion, is necessary for the reformer. A nonviolent organization founded on overt and altruistic principles for the purpose of discussing social issues and agitating for political reform, is a worthwhile action.[38] "A remedy must somewhere have a beginning" (173).

Feeling partially responsible for what he considers Shelley's imprudent, headstrong, and potentially disastrous actions, the worried Godwin sent an immediate response.[39] He told Shelley that he could not divorce himself from any violence that might result from his nonviolent participation in reform. "If you are 'eager that something should be done,' you must take all the consequences of your efforts for that purpose."[40] Because of the long oppression to which they had been subjected, the Irish were seething with hatred and hostility for the English. To awaken them would be dangerous — "their first act will be to destroy each other".[41] If such should occur the guilt would be Shelley's.

Shelley, you are preparing a scene of blood! If your associations take effect to any extensive degree, tremendous consequences will follow, and hundreds, by their calamities and premature fate, will expiate your error. And then what will it avail you to say, "I warned them against this; when I put the seed into the ground, I laid my solemn injunctions upon it, that it should not germinate?"[42]

But Godwin was not presenting Shelley with a moral problem which the young reformer had not considered before. In the "Ad-

---

[38] Shelley's Association was to go beyond simple discussion of problems; it was to be an active agent in producing beneficial change. In the *Weekly Messenger* Shelley had written: "I propose an Association for the following purposes: first, of debating on the propriety of whatever measures may be agitated; and, secondly, for carrying, by united and individual exertion, such measures into effect when determined on." As quoted by Godwin in his letter of March 14 to Shelley, Hogg, 329.

[39] "If you had never read my book you would probably never have gone to Ireland upon the errand that has led you thither. I shall ever regret this effect of my book...." Godwin's March 14 letter to Shelley, Hogg, 330.

[40] *Ibid.*

[41] *Ibid.*

[42] Hogg, 331.

dress" Shelley had written: "Do I do evil, that good may come?
. . . The wisdom and charity of which I speak, are the *only* means
which I will countenance, for the redress of your grievances, and
the grievances of the world. So far as they operate, I am willing
to stand responsible for their *evil* effects" (V, 244). There were
two approaches open to Shelley to actively demonstrate his commitment to the Irish problem. His commitment to nonviolent reform had eliminated two of the most typically human responses
– controlled apathy and violent revolution. Shelley's choices
were: to do as Godwin recommended, speak of political truth in
a generalized way, as *Political Justice* did, and thereby "irrigate
and fertilize the intellectual soil";[43] or to follow the dictates of his
aroused spirit, and apply moral truth to a particular political situation, consider the Irish workingman as a viable political force,
and recommend nonviolent resistance, much as Gandhi in India
would later do. From Plato to Rousseau and from the New Testament to Godwin, the intellectual soil had been adequately fertilized.
In addition to fertilizer, Shelley's contribution to the pursuit of
truth would include a plough. From the revolutionary thought of
a Rousseau and a Godwin springs the revolutionary experience
of a Shelley and a Gandhi. We live the means not the goals. In a
relative world, one's experiments with truth are his truth. Shelley's ideal program for action as expressed in the "Address to
the Irish People" combines the humanistic principles of thinkers
from Plato to Godwin with the nonviolent experience of an individual willing to accept as his own burden the suffering which
social change might temporarily bring to men, in a way that attempts to make the experience of human conflict a beneficial
human enterprise in terms of the individual's understanding of
the human condition. For modern man, likewise confronted with
social injustice, such experience is the best answer to the pragmatic question – Why waste time working for justice when my
actions will produce little result in my own lifetime toward changing the social climate?

To contrast Shelley with Godwin in this way is not to dispar-

[43]   *Ibid.*

age Godwin – a philosopher who certainly was committed to social reform. Shelley simply presents an alternative to the tactics
for reform suggested in *Political Justice*. The subsequent history
of Ireland has vindicated Godwin's prediction: "their first act
will be to destroy each other." A similar tragedy has occurred in
India – where as soon as Gandhi's nonviolent struggle had assured India her independence, the Indians fell to slaughtering
each other. But as Gandhi and Shelley would be quick to
point out – the failure was not with *Satyagraha* but with the *Satyagrahis*. Must such failure inevitably be the result "as long
as men are men"? Shelley's and Gandhi's experiments with truth
deny that they would or could believe such an idea. To them,
the result would be different as men would become men.

But Shelley the nonviolent reformer was about to undergo a
radical change in terms of tactical commitment. A knowledge of
historical circumstance is a prerequisite to nonviolent action. In
spite of adequate fertilizer, the time was not ripe. Shelley's experiment in Ireland, in terms of practical results, was a failure. His
method was not wrong but the situation for its employment did not
exist. Shelley writes to Godwin:

I have withdrawn from circulation the publications wherein I erred
& am preparing to quit Dublin: It is not because I think that *such*
associations as I conceived would be deleterious, that I have withdrawn them. It is possible to festinate or retard the progress of human
perfectibility, such associations as I would have recommended would
be calculated to produce the former effect, the refinement of seces-
sions would prevent a fictitious unanimity, as their publicity would
render ineffectual any schemes of violent innovation. . . . My schemes
of organizing the ignorant I confess to be [dangerous and *cancelled*]
ill-timed: I cannot conceive that they were dangerous (176).

He resigns himself to a change of tactics: "But I submit. I shall
address myself no more to the illiterate, I will look to events in
which it will be impossible that I can share, and make myself the
cause of an effect which will take place ages after *I* shall have
moldered into dust" (176). And submit he did. Not to Godwin, but
to circumstance. Although throughout his brief life he continued
to periodically write political tracts, he never again actively parti-

cipated in a social movement as he did in Ireland.[44] He never again spoke at political rallies or dropped political pamphlets on the heads of passersby from his balcony,[45] but his imagination continued to be inspired by the rapidly occurring events of his day – whether the death of Princess Charlotte or the execution of three accused conspirators, whether the Peterloo massacre or George IV's divorce proceedings, whether the fight for freedom in Italy, Greece, Germany, or Spain, or the abolition of slavery. Shelley's political and social awareness was interfused with his personal confrontation with life, and both found imaginative expression in his poetry and prose. His writing now became a means by which to experiment with truth, and through which to communicate to future ages a new method by which truth might not only be known but experienced. In a dynamic world, truth is relative; thus Shelley's view of truth combined with his belief in social organicism directly challenged the static, Newtonian world-view of contemporary Tory statesmen. The distinction of viewpoints is fundamental to understanding the Romantic rebellion.

The experience of his failure in Ireland did not leave Shelley, and it was soon to be imaginatively transformed into poetry. *The Revolt of Islam* is a poem in which a nonviolent revolution led by an idealistic young leader succeeds, only to be defeated in terms of practical political results by an unready world. In terms of the poem the contrast is between what could be and what is. In terms of Shelley's Irish experience the contrast is between what was and what could have been. "I will look to events in which it will be impossible that I can share . . ."

[44]   One commentator sees Shelley's submission as a crucial decision in his life: "The sense of frustration so evident in Shelley's poetry has its root, I believe, in this renunciation of a more active life." Grabo, *The Magic Plant*, 80.
[45]   Grabo, 67. "A little later he endeavored to disseminate them [ideas] by means of toy balloons and by corked bottles containing pamphlets cast into the sea."

IV

THE REVOLT OF ISLAM

> If anything is to be accomplished in this world,
> it must be done by visionaries, by men and
> women who can see the future, and make the
> future because they can see it.
>
> Keir Hardie

> But when thou famous victorie hast wonne,
> And high emongst all knights hast hong thy
> shield,
> Thenceforth the suit of earthly conquest shonne,
>
> And wash thy hands from guilt of bloudy field;
> For bloud can nought but sin, and wars but
> sorrowes yield.
>
> Spenser, *The Faerie Queene*, I, x, 60

> Blessed are those who are persecuted for right-
> eousness' sake, for theirs is the kingdom of
> heaven.
>
> Matthew 5:10

The Revolt of Islam was composed in six months, April to September, 1817, while Shelley and his family were at Marlow in Buckinghamshire.[1] Although this period was not free from troubles and anxiety, especially concerning his health, Shelley's residency at Marlow for the most part was one of the happiest times of his life. He was crushed by the recent court decision that had deprived him of his two children by Harriet, but Shelley, Mary, and their son, William, enjoyed a genuinely close family life. In 1816, after Shelley had learned of Harriet's death, he married Mary Godwin and thereby appeased her estranged father who against his published principles had opposed their "illegal" un-

---

[1] For Shelley's life at Marlow see White, *Shelley*, I, 498-560.

ion.[2] During his stay at Marlow Shelley generally spent the mornings working on his poem, either in his boat on the Thames or under some shade trees in Bisham Wood. The afternoons were often spent in ministering to the poor – distributing food and clothing, attending the sick, and attempting to defeat despair by spreading hope. In the evening he would read aloud to Mary, to Clare Clairmont who was living with them, and often to a visiting friend or two. Primarily he read the poetry of Spenser and works on the French Revolution – the former artistically and the latter thematically related to the poem he was composing.

The Revolt of Islam is written in Spenserian stanzas, and following the epic style of Spenser is divided into twelve cantos. Encompassing almost five thousand lines, it is Shelley's longest poem. Byron's use of the Spenserian stanza in *Child Harold's Pilgrimage* may have first attracted Shelley to the form.[3] Shelley himself states in a letter to Godwin that "the Poem was produced by a series of thoughts which filled" his mind "with an unbounded and sustained enthusiasm" (432). *The Revolt* is an uneven poem containing some of the most magnificent poetry that Shelley ever wrote, but likewise, and perhaps too often, containing some of the worst. It is marred by a confused plot-line, frequent obscurity, needless repetition, poor melodrama, and overdone sentiment. But where the poem succeeds, it succeeds with genius and grandeur – portraits of men and women struggling with almost superhuman courage against the forces of oppression, vivid descriptions of the horrors of war and of war's aftermath, and forceful dramatization of the author's prophetic vision of "human power".

In composing *The Revolt* Shelley recreated and expanded many of the themes presented in his previous poetic endeavors, especially *Queen Mab* and "Alastor".[4] The principal themes of *Queen*

---

[2]   Reiter, *A Study of Shelley's Poetry*, 55.
[3]   Donald H. Reiman, *Percy Bysshe Shelley* (New York: Twayne Publishers, Inc., 1969), 52.
[4]   Floyd Stovall sees a biographical motivation for the poem. "Lord Eldon's judgment depriving him of the care of Harriet's children was delivered near the end of March, 1817, and *Laon and Cythna* was begun within the

Mab, the hatred of oppression and the love of freedom, are restated in *The Revolt* with noticeable improvement in artistic finesse. Shelley the poet no longer attempts to preach truth "didactically", but rather through an imaginative "narrative" to attain "the power of awakening in others sensations like those which animate" his own "bosom".[5] Also, there is good evidence that in one sense Shelley wrote *The Revolt* as a sequel to "Alastor".[6] In Canto I the female spirit of hope recounts her first contact with "divinest lore".

> A dying poet gave me books, and blessed
> With wild but holy talk the sweet unrest
> In which I watched him as he died away –
> A youth with hoary hair – a fleeting guest
> Of our lone mountains: and this lore did sway
> My spirit like a storm, contending there alway.
>
> (ll. 454-9)

The poet in "Alastor" descended "to an untimely grave" because of his "self-centered seclusion" from humanity, and because of his egoistic and other-worldly search for his "prototype" (I, 173). He erred in forsaking human love (the Arab-maiden) and brotherhood (the cottagers), and in attempting to discover an ethereal existence by escaping from the conflicts of his earthbound humanity. Whereas the quest of the Alastor poet ends in frustration and failure, the quest of Laon, the equally sensitive

---

succeeding two or three weeks. To say that the result of the suit in Chancery was the genesis of the poem would be unwarranted conjecture, but there can be little doubt that his propensity to look upon himself as a martyr who returned good for the evil he received at the hands of society was increased by this new punishment inflicted upon him; and it would be natural for him, still returning good for evil, to make in poetry the sacrifice for humanity which was impossible in actual life" (*Desire and Restraint in Shelley,* 151-2).

[5] "'Preface' to *The Revolt of Islam*", *Shelley: Poetical Works,* ed. Thomas Hutchinson (London: Oxford University Press, 1967), 32-5. All further references to *The Revolt of Islam* are to this edition, and will be given by line numbers within the text. Hutchinson prints the revised edition of the poem, while the Julian Edition prints only the original edition.

[6] Donald H. Reiman, *Shelley's "The Triumph of Life": A Critical Study* (Urbana: University of Illinois Press, 1965), 20.

poet in *The Revolt of Islam,* ends in happiness and success. Laon responds to human love and gives his existence eternal meaning through involvement in the temporal conflicts of mankind. The different perspectives on the poet as presented in these two poems represent two opposing elements in the psychological make-up of Shelley himself – the urge to withdraw into a mystical search for fulfillment, and the urge to find fulfillment through commitment to social justice. Shelley consistently chose the role of Laon, the poet who communicates truth and hope to men. Indeed, this is Shelley's position as the author of "Alastor" – that is why the poem "is not barren of instruction to actual men" (I, 173).[7]

The French Revolution, and his extensive reading about it, provided Shelley with additional source material for his poem.[8] His discussion of the French Revolution in the "Preface" to *The Revolt,* his specific delineation of its causes, tactics, results, and his belief in the despair it produced in contemporaries (Wordsworth, Coleridge, Southey), suggests that Shelley wanted his readers to make the connection between the actual revolution and his imaginary one, and in the contrast between the two discover the political, moral, and human truths that he was attempting to communicate. Such a discovery on the part of individual readers would create once again an atmosphere in which men "thirst for a happier condition of moral and political society" (Preface). The next call to action would then find men who had learned from the

---

[7] Grabo, *The Magic Plant,* 173. "Shelley [in "Alastor"] is contemplating the possible fate of such a one as himself, sensitive of spirit, who withdraws from the harsh conflicts of life, as he was himself tempted to do, and loses himself in a world of dream and illusion, pursuant of an ideal not to be realized in earthly form. That Shelley was fully conscious of such a temptation indicates his superiority to it, a superiority not maintained without conflict to the end of his days."

[8] For a thorough investigation of Shelley's attitude toward the French Revolution, especially as historical background for *The Revolt of Islam,* see Amiyakumar Sen, *Studies in Shelley,* 271-335. "The excesses of the terror [in French Revolution] had sunk deep into his sensitive mind. They did not indeed shake his belief in the innate goodness of human nature nor his firm conviction that the principles which seemed to be submerged by such tempestuous proceedings were sure to triumph in the end. They simply strengthened his innate reverence for non-violence, and increased his disgust for ill-regulated passions" (304-5).

experience of the French Revolution, and who had learned from the experience of Shelley's historicizing.[9]

The pervading spirit of *The Revolt of Islam* is the ethical supposition that one should return good for evil. At this time Shelley was reading the moral teaching of Jesus Christ, and the spirit of the Sermon on the Mount underlies the motivation of the poem's hero and heroine.[10] Leigh Hunt states that for his Christianity, "in the proper sense of the word", Shelley "went to the Epistle of St. James, and to the Sermon on the Mount by Christ himself."[11] Given Shelley's commitment to virtue and justice, one can easily understand why he would be attracted to a system of ethics that prophesied: "Blessed are those who hunger and thirst for righteousness, for they shall be satisfied" (Matt. 5:6).

In the "Preface" Shelley states that *The Revolt of Islam* was written to the "enlightened and refined". His purpose was that of the poet – "to communicate to others the pleasure and the enthusiasm arising out of those images and feelings in the vivid presence of which within his own mind consists at once his inspiration and his reward" (Preface). His purpose was that of the social reformer – to excite the imagination and sympathy of the public by the presentation of a "*beau ideal*" revolution (417). The *beau ideal* revolution is one of nonviolence, one of love.

> In recommending also a great and important change in the spirit which animates the social institutions of mankind, I have avoided all flattery to those violent and malignant passions of our nature which are ever on the watch to mingle with and to alloy the most beneficial innovations. There is no quarter given to Revenge, or Envy, or Prejudice. Love is celebrated everywhere as the sole law which should govern the moral world (Preface).

In this chapter we will concentrate on discovering Shelley's attitude toward nonviolence as it is expressed in this poem. Such a

---

[9] Shelley's historical sensibility can be considered perceptive in terms of Freud's psychoanalytic theory as interpreted and disseminated by Erik H. Erikson. "I mean to say ... that man by understanding the way he historicizes may yet overcome certain stereotyped ways in which history repeats itself – ways which man can no longer afford" (*Gandhi's Truth*, 439).

[10] Grabo, 224.

[11] *The Autobiography of Leigh Hunt*, 269.

focus may unavoidably distort the total meaning of the poem, but such an analysis is valid if it contributes to our understanding of how nonviolence operates in the poem, and how it operates in Shelley's political and ethical thought. *The Revolt of Islam* was not written to be a well-organized, nonviolent handbook, but rather to provoke the thoughts and feelings of its readers into identification with Laon and Cythna and their cause – the quest for the ideal society through nonviolent means. To the extent that we make their cause our cause, and their means our means, Shelley has fulfilled his purpose in writing the poem.

1

The Revolt of Islam begins with a poetic dedication to Mary, in which Shelley briefly reviews his personal struggle against tyranny, and sings a hymn to Mary for the inspiration that she has given in his battle. Thus imaginatively the poet identifies Mary and himself with the heroine and hero of his poem, Cythna and Laon. Shelley praises Mary for her "sweetest smiles" and "gentle speech" and declares that he sees the "lamp of vestal power" burning in her soul. He also praises Mary's parents, Mary Wollstonecraft and William Godwin, for their ardent crusades in behalf of social justice. Mary Wollstonecraft and William Godwin are thematically linked to the central concerns of *The Revolt of Islam,* just as Shelley and Mary are prophetically and dramatically linked to those concerns. In the poem Cythna, in the spirit of Mary Wollstonecraft, champions a movement for the liberation of women; and Laon, in the spirit of William Godwin, is committed to the doctrine of human perfectibility. Mary and Shelley, as Cythna and Laon, through their commitment to social justice will find permanence in a world of flux, and immortality in a world of time.

> Truth's deathless voice pauses among mankind!
>   If there must be no response to my cry –
> If men must rise and stamp with fury blind
>   On his pure name who loves them, – thou and I,
>   Sweet friend! can look from our tranquility

Like lamps into the world's tempestuous night, –
Two tranquil stars, while clouds are passing by
Which wrap them from the foundering seaman's sight,
That burn from year to year with unextinguished light.

(ll. 118-26)

The first canto of the poem is "introductory" (Preface), and "in some measure a distinct poem, tho' very necessary to the wholeness of the work" (417). It is integrated thematically and symbolically with the eleven cantos that follow, which constitute the main story-line of the poem. Shelley's persona, the poet of the poem, is introduced grappling with the meaning and significance of the French Revolution; he has survived "the age of despair" and has become aware "of a slow, gradual, silent change" (Preface) in the destiny of man. The poem as a whole builds a crescendo to this belief, and concludes with an affirmation that the "golden dawn" has arrived.

Standing on the seashore, the poet views the struggle high overhead between the Serpent and the Eagle. The struggle symbolically represents the continuous battle between the spirit of good, the Serpent, whose heavenly shape is the Morning Star, and the spirit of evil, the Eagle, whose heavenly shape is the blood-red Comet.[12] Shelley purposely inverts traditional symbols of good and evil in order to symbolically represent mankind's mistaken notions of what is good and what is evil. Although man frequently has not been able to distinguish the good forces in existence from the evil ones, this struggle has existed throughout history, and is the primary conflict in Laon's and Cythna's story. To Shelley, the spirit of evil is not synonymous with the general orthodox conceptions of "devil" and "sin", but rather represents the tyranny of despots, the oppression of churches, and individual man's potential for hate, violence, and selfishness. It derives power from man's own ignorance. Similarly, the spirit of good should not be considered as the traditional obedience to authority, but rather it represents the freedom and equality of all human beings, and the individual's potential for love, nonviolence, and brotherhood. Its

---

[12] Stovall, *Desire and Restraint in Shelley*, 159-60.

principal power is man's imagination. Elsewhere, Shelley calls this spirit "Intellectual Beauty".

At the conclusion of the violent struggle for supremacy, the apparently lifeless Serpent falls into the sea, and the battered but victorious Eagle flies away. But a woman, who represents Hope, finds the crippled but not fatally wounded Serpent, and nurses it on her breast. The poet joins them and they set sail in a boat, which is Love, to the Temple of Immortality. On the way she explains to the poet the meaning of what has just occurred – the age-old battle between good and evil. The history of man began with this struggle.

> "The earliest dweller of the world, alone,
>   Stood on the verge of chaos. Lo! afar
> O'er the wide wild abyss two meteors shone,
>   Sprung from the depth of its tempestuous jar:
>   A blood-red Comet and the Morning Star
> Mingling their beams in combat – as he stood,
>   All thoughts within his mind waged mutual war,
>   In dreadful sympathy – when to the flood
> That fair Star fell, he turned and shed his brother's blood.
>
> "Thus evil triumphed, and the Spirit of evil,
>   One Power of many shapes which none may know,
> One Shape of many names; the Fiend did revel
>   In victory, reigning o'er a world of woe,
>   For the new race of man went to and fro,
> Famished and homeless, loathed and loathing, wild,
>   And hating good – for his immortal foe,
>   He changed from starry shape, beauteous and mild,
> To a dire Snake, with man and beast unreconciled."

(ll. 361–78)

When Cain murdered his brother Abel, man fell and came under the Spirit of evil. Thus man has been murdering his brother ever since. It is important to notice Shelley's unorthodox interpretation of Biblical history. Man's first evil act was not Adam and Eve's disobedience of authority, but rather the first violent act of brother against brother. But "Fear, Hatred, Faith, and Tyranny" have distorted the truth, and snared their "subtle nets" around "the living and the dead" (ll. 386–7). The tyrants of despotism have changed the Spirit of good into a lowly Serpent, and have declared it to be the sign of man's disobedience to authority and, as such, the curse of man's fall and the root of all evil.

> "And the great Spirit of Good did creep among
> The nations of mankind, and every tongue
> Cursed and blasphemed him as he passed; for none
> Knew good from evil, though their names were hung
> In mockery o'er the fane where many a groan,
> As King, and Lord, and God, the conquering Fiend did own."
>
> (ll. 373-8)

Encouraged and enforced by the violent oppression of king and priest, ignorance, fear, and superstition have kept man from the truth. The Spirit of evil reigns supreme in the world, and man in his blindness calls it good.

But, the woman continues to the poet, the Spirit of good has often vied for supremacy in the minds and hearts of men. The struggle between the Serpent and the Eagle which he has just witnessed was the most recent one – the French Revolution. Justice and truth waged silent war with Custom, and priests and kings feared as the world's foundations trembled. Even though it appears that the Spirit of evil has been once again victorious, the poet should not despair.

> "Though thou may'st hear that earth is now become
> The tyrant's garbage, which to his compeers,
> The vile reward of their dishonoured years,
> He will dividing give. – The victor Fiend,
> Omnipotent of yore, now quails, and fears
> His triumph dearly won, which soon will lend
> An impulse swift and sure to his approaching end."
>
> (ll. 426–32)

Hope and the Spirit of good have gone forth into the hearts and minds of men. Kings and priests sit upon tarnished thrones. A moral revolution is at hand. The empathic imagination, the weapon of the poet and the reformer, has been stirred and vitalized.[13]

> "My heart was pierced with sympathy, for woe
> Which could not be mine own." (ll. 438-9)

[13] For the role of the empathic imagination in Shelley's theory of poetry see Robert Damm, "A Tale of Human Power: Art and Life in Shelley's Poetic Theory", Unpublished Dissertation, Miami University, 1970.

. . . .

"For I loved all things with intense devotion."

(l. 465)

When people imaginatively comprehend the Spirit of good, of love, of nonviolence, then the ideal revolution is accomplished. The weapons of despots – fear, gold, violence – will cease to be effective; thrones will lose their lustre, and no one will come forward to polish them.

As the Morning Star rises in the heavens, the little boat sails into the Temple of Immortality. The poet then hears the story of two spirits, Laon and Cythna, recently arrived from battle in the temporal world. They are two who on time-bound earth imaginatively comprehended the Spirit of good, and who as poets attempted to develop the empathic imagination in all people and thus revolutionize man's world. Their story, the subject matter of the poem's subsequent cantos, is one of success and of failure; its meaning is hope.

2

Laon begins by telling of his childhood and of the misery that engulfed his native land, Argolis.

> The land in which I lived, by a fell bane
>   Was withered up. Tyrants dwelt side by side,
> And stabled in our homes, – until the chain
>   Stifled the captive's cry, and to abide
>   That blasting curse men had no shame – all vied
> In evil, slave and despot; fear with lust
>   Strange fellowship through mutual hate had tied,
> Like two dark serpents tangled in the dust,
> Which on the paths of men their mingling poison thrust.

(ll. 694-702)

Laon asserts a belief that is familiar in Shelley's poetry. All tyranny is a conspiracy of despot and slave. The slave gives the despot the power by which he tyrannizes, and participates in tyranny's guilt by contributing to the evil.

> For they all pined in bondage; body and soul,
>   Tyrant and slave, victim and torturer, bent
> Before one Power, to which supreme control
>   Over their will be their own weakness leant,
>   Made all its many names omnipotent.

(ll. 730-4)

The imaginative realization that both tyrant and slave are equally chained to the pillar of hatred and violence is the initial premise of the nonviolent activist; it is a premise that Laon can now state, but it is one that he has come to fully understand only through his experiences in time. One motivation that distinguishes the violent radical from the nonviolent revolutionary is that the former usually seeks revenge on his oppressor, while the latter seeks to love his enemy. It is the new law that must replace the old one if mankind is to survive in freedom and justice – if mankind is to survive.

You have heard that it was said, "You shall love your neighbor and hate your enemy." But I say to you, Love your enemies and pray for those who persecute you (Matt. 5:43-44).

Our criticism will therefore be if we *believe* him to be guilty of untruth to meet it with truth, of discourtesy with courtesy, of bullying with calm courage, of violence with suffering, of arrogance with humility, of evil with good.[14]

Here, then, is a truly revolutionary means to a revolutionary end. Because it is often misunderstood it needs emphasis. For example, Joseph Barrell in his book *Shelley and the Thought of His Time* considers Shelley's merging of Christian ethics with radical political goals as a lessening of his revolutionary fervor.

Yet one wonders if ethics and radicalism really mix, if Shelley's advance as a moralist is not a sign of his permanent decline as a radical. For it is noticeable that the belief in the parity of good and evil takes the punch out of the radical speeches of Laon and Cythna. ... We notice a weakening of the radical fervor, a recourse to supposition [love? nonviolence?] unknown to the true radical. The true radical is an *espirit simpliste*. He fails to see why the potential mood should be used at all. "Off with their heads! To the lantern! Stamp out the infamous thing!" ... Thus we notice in *The Revolt of Islam*

[14] Gandhi, *Non-Violent Resistance*, 84.

a new awareness of the problem of evil. It is present both to Shelley and his characters. It is present, however, as a stumbling block, and receives no solution. Its presence, as a matter of fact, invalidates most, if not all, of the radical thinking of the poem.[15]

Barrell is correct in stating that Shelley was an ethicist, but it does not follow that therefore he was not a radical. Laon and Cythna do not countenance revenge and violence, but this does not mean that therefore the movement they lead is not revolutionary in word and deed.[16] Like Jesus before him and Gandhi after him, Shelley mixes political radicalism and moral philosophy. He recognizes the existence of evil. He also recognizes that it is through the dynamics of good and evil in the human psyche and in human interrelationships that identity is defined, and through which reform is wrought.[17] It is a moral vision similar to William Blake's dynamics of opposites in which good can only be realized through its confrontation with evil.[18] Jerusalem, like the Utopia of Prometheus, is a state of existence in which all men realize the good, but in which evil is not extinguished. In the world of Laon and Cythna, evil's interaction with good in experience gives man the potential to break the barriers of time. If Laon had acted as Barrell would have the revolutionary act – sought revenge, and fought violence with violence – he would have failed miserably, and most im-

[15] *Shelley and the Thought of His Time* (New Haven: Yale University Press, 1947), 136-8.
[16] Lest I be accused of semantic bickering with Barrell, to my way of thinking the following statement by Gandhi is radical advice to give to the oppressed: "You are no *satyagrahis* if you remain silent or passive spectators while your enemy is being done to death. You must protect him even at the cost of your own life" (*Gandhi On Non-Violence*, 58). Laon, in Canto V, at the risk of his life protects the tyrant Othman.
[17] Gandhi was an ethicist in basically the same way Shelley was. "Gandhi had identified truth with God. Betokening an uneasiness in the realm of theological dogmatism, he expressed the God of his conception in terms relative to limitless individual interpretations. When conflict resulted, he resorted to the dynamics of human interrelationships for criteria to judge the truth, or its approximation, in a given situation. This led him, necessarily, back to the realm of ethics. To an understanding of the ethical implications of his basic metaphysic, and to action based upon them, Gandhi dedicated his life" (Joan Bondurant, *Conquest of Violence*, 22-3).
[18] Compare Gandhi: "The virtues of mercy, non-violence, love and truth in any man can be truly tested only when pitted against ruthlessness, violence, hate and untruth" (*Gandhi On Non-Violence*, 31).

portant, he would not have found salvation in the Temple of Immortality. And in another sense, had Laon acted with violence against his oppressors, he would have been a sound traditionalist – one who acts as the oppressors expect a revolutionary to act, as the oppressors themselves act. In Shelley, as in the modern world, we should not associate radicalism with violence.

Cythna, at age twelve, like Christ in the temple, is wise beyond her years. She is an orphan raised as Laon's sister,[19] and together they have studied the ways of man and of nature, and mutually inspired each other. As Laon has seen the paradoxical relationship between tyrant and slave, Cythna sees the parallel one between man and woman. "Can man be free if woman be a slave?" (l. 1045).

> "It shall be mine
> This task, mine Laon! – thou hast much to gain;
> Nor wilt thou at poor Cythna's pride repine,
> If she should lead a happy female train
> To meet thee over the rejoicing plain,
> When myriads at thy call shall throng around
> The Golden City." (ll. 1000-6)

Laon and Cythna dedicate themselves to the cause of freedom and justice for all men and women – to be committed poet-leaders.

In the third canto Laon and Cythna awake to find themselves surrounded by "armed men" in the midst of a general purge of dissidents; on orders from the tyrant many people are slaughtered and others sold into slavery. As Cythna is being carried off into slavery, Laon hears her cry for help. He discovers her, and she exhorts him to remember what he has said about man's common humanity, about slaves and tyrants.

---

[19] In the first edition of the poem, entitled *Laon and Cythna,* the two "were brother and sister, who loved each other without benefit of clergy" (White, *Shelley* I, 549). A few copies of the first edition had been circulated when in December, 1817, the Olliers, Shelley's publishers, withdrew it from circulation. They refused to publish the book unless Shelley made changes in the poem where certain social and religious mores were affronted. Shelley complied, and the poem was published as *The Revolt of Islam* early in 1818. For a thorough discussion of Shelley's relations with his publishers at this time, consult White, *Shelley*, I, 547-52.

> "Look not so Laon – say farewell in hope,
> 　　These bloody men are but the slaves who bear
> Their mistress to her task – it was my scope
> 　　The slavery where they drag me now, to share,
> 　　And among captives willing chains to wear
> Awhile – the rest thou knowest – return, dear friend!
> 　　Let our first triumph trample the despair
> Which would ensnare us now, for in the end,
> In victory or in death our hopes and fears must blend."

(ll. 1180-8)

But Laon is incensed.

> These words had fallen on my unheeding ear,
> 　　Whilst I had watched the motions of the crew
> With seeming-careless glance; not many were
> 　　Around her, for their comrades just withdrew
> 　　To guard some other victim – so I drew
> My knife, and with one impulse, suddenly
> 　　All unaware three of their number slew,
> And grasped a fourth by the throat, and with loud cry
> My countrymen invoked to death or liberty!

(ll. 1089-97)

Here is Barrell's radical. It is a familiar picture. It is also a realistic one. In fear and desperation Laon forgets the truths that he had taught Cythna, and acts violently out of hatred and despair. His acts are futile. He is granted neither "death" nor "liberty". He is taken to a cave above the city and chained to a pillar overlooking the sea. There he watches the ship that carries Cythna into slavery slowly sail out of his sight. For four days and nights he suffers despair, hunger, thirst, and insanity. Laon suffers for his sin against humanity; he experiences physical agony and spiritual anguish. Near death, he is rescued by a "Hermit old" and they set sail for a faraway island.

Canto IV takes place on the island. The Hermit has cared for Laon, and the young radical has physically and mentally been healed, and spiritually been made whole again. For seven years he has read the great philosophers and poets of past ages and has benefited from the wisdom of the old Hermit. The Hermit has told Laon how he was able to free him.

He came to the lone column on the rock
  And with his sweet and mighty eloquence
The hearts of those who watched it did unlock,
  And made them melt in tears of penitence.
  They gave him entrance free to bear me thence.

(ll. 1504-8)

The situation in which the Hermit rescued Laon was similar to
the one which Laon faced in attempting to rescue Cythna. The
Hermit also tells Laon of a young woman revolutionary, named
Laone, who in Argolis is leading a "gentle" revolution in behalf of woman's freedom and justice. She too had escaped slavery.

  And with these quiet words – "For thine own sake
I prithee spare me;" – did with ruth so take

  All hearts, that even the torturer who had bound
  Her meek calm frame, ere it was yet impaled,
Loosened her, weeping then; nor could be found
  One human hand to harm her – unassailed
  Therefore she walks through the great City.

(ll. 1574-80)

Laone is, of course, Cythna. Her freedom ironically demonstrates
the futility of Laon's murder of the soldiers. The Hermit's and
Laone's actions are directly contrasted with the irrational and in-
human actions of Laon. Each of the three were faced with a similar situation, and the two situations in which nonviolent means
were employed resulted in the successful release of the respective captives. In both cases, the Hermit's and Laone's, there was
a nonviolent success *beau ideal* in that not only was the objective
of freeing the prisoner accomplished, but the enemy "slaves"
were converted through imaginative understanding to the side of
truth and justice.[20] Shelley artistically juxtaposes these three situations, and the meaning of the incidents is not lost to Laon. He

[20] Gandhi's faith in humanity was similar to Shelley's: "Whether we may
think he succeeded or failed, Gandhi never ceased to believe in the possibility of a love of truth so strong and so pure that it would leave an 'in-
delible impress' upon the most recalcitrant enemy, and awaken in him a
response of love and truth" (Thomas Merton, "Introduction", *Gandhi On
Non-Violence*, 19).

now realizes that a "belief in nonviolence is based on the assumption that human nature in its essence is one and therefore unfailingly responds to advances to love".[21] He has developed a philosophy of action – one that will be soon experientially tested. As Laon goes off to help Laone in the nonviolent revolution (secretly hoping that Laone might be Cythna), he will recall how the Hermit and Laone changed the hearts and minds of individual men, and he will employ the same techniques in mass action. The last words of the Hermit to Laon are prophetic:

> "If blood be shed, 'tis but a change and choice
>   Of bonds, – from slavery to cowardice
> A wretched fall! – Uplift thy charmed voice!
>   Pour on those evil men the love that lies
>   Hovering within those spirit soothing eyes –
> Arise, my friend, farewell!"
>
> (ll. 1657-62)

3

Shortly after Laon reaches the camp of Laone's followers, the army of the tyrant secretly murders ten thousand of the Patriots in their sleep. In the confusion and alarm that follow the Patriots shout the name of "Laon" as a rallying cry. They regroup and quickly surround the "false murderers", when "revenge and fear / Made the high virtue of the patriots fail" (ll. 1788-9). In despair at the horror of the experience, one patriot reacts as Laon has once done.

> One pointed on his foe the mortal spear –
> I rushed before its point, and cried, "Forbear, forbear!"
>
> The spear transfixed my arm that was uplifted
>   In swift expostulation, and the blood
> Gushed round its point.
>
> (ll. 1790-4)

Laon steps in and takes the blow intended for the enemy. He now understands that a virtuous cause must use only virtuous means – that violence and revenge are wrong. He has also come

---

[21] Mahatma Gandhi, as quoted by James W. Douglas in his book *The Non-Violent Cross* (London: Macmillan, 1969), p. 86.

to recognize the conciliatory power of suffering – of suffering for your enemies' sins – and he seizes the moment to unshield the nonviolent weapons he has obtained under the tutelage of the Hermit: the power of truth, of word, of personality, of moral superiority, and of forgiveness of sins.[22]

"Soldiers, our brethren and our friends are slain.
  Ye murdered them, I think, as they did sleep!
Alas, what have ye done? the slightest pain
  Which ye might suffer, there were eyes to weep,
  But ye have quenched them – there were smiles to steep
Your hearts in balm, but they are lost in woe;
  And those whom love did set his watch to keep
Around your tents, truth's freedom to bestow,
Ye stabbed as they did sleep – but they forgive ye now.

"Oh wherefore should ill ever flow from ill,
  And pain still keener pain for ever breed?
We all are brethren – even the slaves who kill
  For hire, are men; and two avenge misdeed
  On the misdoer, doth but Misery feed
With her own broken heart! O Earth, O Heaven!
  And thou, dread Nature, which to every deed
And all that lives or is, to be hath given,
Even as to thee have these done ill, and are forgiven!

"Join then your hands and hearts, and let the past
  Be as a grave which gives not up its dead
To evil thoughts." – A film then overcast
  My sense with dimness, for the wound, which bled
  Freshly, swift shadows o'er mine eyes had shed.
When I awoke, I lay mid friends and foes,
  And earnest countenances on me shed
The light of questioning looks, whilst one did close
My wound with balmiest herbs, and soothed me to repose;

And one whose spear had pierced me, leaned beside,
  With quivering lips and humid eyes; – and all
Seemed like some brothers on a journey wide
  Gone forth, whom now strange meeting did befall

[22] Compare Martin Luther King's essay "Letters from Birmingham Jail", in *Why We Can't Wait* (New York: Harper and Row, 1963), 77-100. "Over the past few years I have consistently preached that nonviolence demands that the means we use be as pure as the ends we seek" (98).

In a strange land, round one whom they might call
Their friend, their chief, their father, for assay
Of peril, which had saved them from the thrall
Of death, now suffering. Thus the vast array
Of those fraternal bands were reconciled that day.

Lifting the thunder of their acclamation,
   Towards the City then the multitude,
And I among them, went in joy – a nation
   Made free by love; – a mighty brotherhood
   Linked by a jealous interchange of good;
A glorious pageant, more magnificent
   Than kingly slaves arrayed in gold and blood,
When they return from carnage, and are sent
In triumph bright beneath the populous battlement.

(ll. 1801-45)

This is the new army for the new society.

I have quoted the preceding section at length because it is a poetic dramatization of the nonviolent revolutionary experience, of the "human power" of "sublime intent", and of the conciliatory power of love. When one becomes committed to the cause of social justice for all men, and is prepared to suffer for it, he confirms his own humanity. And as Cesar Chavez has said recently, when one makes his commitment nonviolent, he confirms the humanity of all men.[23] Shelley's purpose in portraying this event was not to make it realistically credible, but rather to "awaken the feelings" of the reader so that he may imaginatively experience "the beauty of true virtue" (Preface). His purpose was not to dramatize the revolutionary experience as it has existed, but as it might and should exist. His purpose was to preserve the future through an imaginative interpretation of the past. In other words, Shelley realized that the way men responded to interpretations of history would influence their actions in the events of the future. Therefore, one of the ways to break the cycle of violence responding to violence as history repeats itself, is to interpret the future by imaginatively reconstructing the past as Shelley has done in *The Revolt of Islam*. It is to change the historical view of man as a creature limited by his instinctual behavior to a prophetic view of man

[23] "Nonviolence in a Good Cause", *Fellowship* (July 1970), 21-2.

as a being capable of breaking the historical cycles that bind him. Such is the meaning of the poet's cry at the conclusion of *Hellas*.

> Oh, cease! must hate and death return?
>   Cease! must men kill and die?
> Cease! drain not to its dregs the urn
>   Of bitter prophecy.
> The world is weary of the past,
>   Oh, might it die or rest at last!

(III, 53)

The new nonviolent army of peace and brotherhood, with Laon at its head, now turns and advances on the Golden City. They are determined by active nonviolent aggression to attain freedom and justice. In the city the people are jubilant; despite the enormous number who have joined the revolution, none wants for food or shelter, for each citizen shares with his brother.

>   – Therefore to the gate
> Of the Imperial House, now desolate,
> I passed, and there was found aghast, alone,
>   The fallen Tyrant! – Silently he sate,
> Upon the footstool of his golden throne,
>   Which, starred with sunny gems, in its own lustre shone.

(ll. 1894-9)

The *beau ideal* revolution is completed. The power of the tyrant is gone. The people have simply willed not to be slaves and the enslaving chains of fear have fallen from them. The tyrant has only the power the slaves give to him, and now they have withdrawn their cooperation with evil. But while the king has no power, he is not unloved. A little child, Cythna's daughter as we discover later, recognizes Othman's humanity and thus his potential for good. But the people of the city do not, and when they see the powerless monarch, they turn into an angry mob that demands vengeance in the name of justice.

> Then was heard – "He who judged let him be brought
>   To judgement! blood for blood cries from the soil
> On which his crimes had deep pollution wrought!
> Shall Othman only unavenged despoil?
>   Shall they who by the stress of grinding toil
> Wrest from the unwilling earth his luxuries,

> Perish for crime, while his foul blood may boil,
> Or creep within his veins at will? – Arise!
> And to high justice make her chosen sacrifice."
>
> (ll. 1999-2007)

The mob understands only the old law – only an eye for an eye
justice. Laon speaks:

> "What do ye seek? what fear ye," then I cried,
>   Suddenly starting forth, "that ye should shed
> The blood of Othman?"   (ll. 2008-10)
> . . . .
> "What call ye *justice*? Is there one who ne'er
>   In secret thought has wished another's ill? –
> Are ye all pure? Let those stand forth who hear,
>   And tremble not. Shall they insult and kill,
> If such they be? their mild eyes can they fill
> With false anger of the hypocrite?
>   Alas, such were not pure, – the chastened will
> Of virtue sees that justice is the light
> Of love, and not revenge, and terror and despite."
>
> (ll. 2017-25)

"He that is without sin among you, let him cast the first stone"
(John 8:7).[24] And as in the Biblical story, the crowd desists. They
begin to pity the former tyrant. Laon has again changed the course
of revolution by demanding the use of only nonviolent means.
Once again Laon's power is his imagination's comprehension of
the potential for good in his fellow man and his weapons are
truth, reason, and poetry – the weapons which can change the
minds and hearts of men. Indeed, Shelley's insights in this regard
are surprisingly contemporary. Rosemary Reuther in a recent article has written:

We must rise from the level of wrath to that of an angry love, even
for the worst of our adversaries. For whenever the cry "kill the pig" is

[24] In his letter to Southey, August 17, 1820, Shelley again uses this parable
– this time to berate the self-proclaimed "moral high-mindedness" of the
laureate. "Instead, therefore, of refraining from 'judging that you be not
judged,' you not only judge but condemn, and that to a punishment which
its victim must be either among the meanest or loftiest not to regard as
bitterer than death. But you are such a pure one as Jesus Christ found not
in all Judea to throw the first stone against the woman taken in adultery!"
(583)

raised, we not only confine the possibilities of the adversary to the level of the beast, but we ourselves inevitably sink to the same level. To dehumanize the enemy is ultimately to assure your own dehumanization as well and to destroy the foundation of the revolution. "Love your enemy." This means nothing less than to be as jealous for the reclamation of the humanity of your adversary as you are for your own, even as you uncompromisingly demand his conversion from the bestiality into which he has fallen. Ultimately understood, to love one's enemy is neither utopian nor sentimental, but the only basis on which the revolutionary can be sure to retain his own humanity in the midst of the revolutionary process. Only through this principle can the revolution become a real transformation and not just a reversal of things in which oppressed becomes oppressor and oppressor becomes oppressed. The only revolution which can create a really better world is one which knows profoundly that the liberation of the oppressed must be the liberation of the oppressor as well, and the creation of a new possibility for everyone. This was the vision Martin Luther King held out to us, but neither white America nor Black America was ready for it at that time.[25]

Laon indeed seeks to maintain his "humanity in the midst of the revolutionary process". He seeks to liberate the oppressed and the oppressor by demanding that the revolutionaries "love their enemy", not dehumanize both the enemy and themselves by "revenge, and terror and despite". Laon's actions demonstrate the necessity of a strong and charismatic hero-leader in Shelley's vision of a nonviolent revolution. Only Laon and Cythna, and perhaps their close circle of friends, really understand the philosophy of nonviolence. Under pressure the mass of people strike out with violence at that which they fear. The poet-leader must convince them that they have the power to conquer fear, and through the example of his personal conduct convince the people of the truth of nonviolence. Shelley's portrayal of the unifying power of the nonviolent leader is prophetic when we consider the charismatic leadership of Mahatma Gandhi and Martin Luther King, of Danilo Dolci and Cesar Chavez. When we realize the potential for human fulfillment that Shelley envisioned arising from such leadership, and remember that in Ireland Shelley desired to become such a leader himself and could not, then we can better understand

[25] " 'Love Your Enemies' as Rebellion", *Fellowship* (July, 1970), 8, 23, 30.

the anguish which the poet expresses in "Ode to the West Wind".

> Drive my dead thoughts over the universe
> Like withered leaves to quicken a new birth!
> And, by the incantation of this verse,
>
> Scatter, as from an unextinguished hearth
> Ashes and sparks, my words among mankind!
> Be through my lips to unawakened earth
>
> The trumpet of a prophecy! O, Wind,
> If Winter comes, can Spring be far behind?

(II, 297)

The peace and joy established by the revolution are short lived. The tyrant supported by foreign armies – slaves sent by despots who feared the success of the nonviolent revolution in Argolis – subdue the Patriots through wholesale slaughter. The rallying cry of the people rings in the city.

> "They come! to arms! to arms!
> The Tyrant is amongst us, and the stranger
> Comes to enslave us in his name! to arms!"

(ll. 2354-6)

The multitude react as their training, education, and experience have taught them. When they are threatened by violence, they react with violence. But Laon realizes the futility of such action. Even in the midst of the cruel and bloody slaughter of the Patriots, he attempts to organize nonviolent resistance.

> A band of brothers gathering round me, made,
> Although unarmed, a steadfast front, and still
> Retreating, with stern looks beneath the shade
> Of gathered eyebrows, did the victors fill
> With doubt even in success; deliberate will
> Inspired our growing troop, not overthrown
> It gained the shelter of a grassy hill,
> And ever still our comrades were hewn down,
> And their defenceless limbs beneath our footsteps strown.

(ll. 2407-15)

The "myriads flocked in love and brotherhood to die" (l. 2424).
They willingly offer themselves as a sacrifice to active love, to freedom, to humanity. Then some of the Patriots find "a bundle of
rude pikes" in a cave, with which they futilely arm themselves
against the enemy's superior artillery. But the slaughter continues until Laon alone survives. Just as he is about to be murdered,
Cythna, "robed in white", melodramatically appears on "a black
Tartarian horse of giant frame", and sweeps the "vanquished"
Laon from out of the enemy's grasp, and together they flee to a
mountain retreat.

The scene of the bloody counter-revolution presents a problem
in critical interpretation for our study of nonviolence in Shelley.

> Within a cave upon the hill were found
>   A bundle of rude pikes, the instrument
> Of those who war but on their native ground
>   For natural rights: a shout of joyance sent
>   Even from our hearts the wide air pierced and rent,
> As those few arms the bravest and the best
>   Seized, and each sixth, thus armed, did now present
> A line which covered and sustained the rest,
> A confident phalanx, which the foe on every side invest.
>
>   (ll. 2443-51)

As Laon and his followers turn to their rude weapons, two questions immediately arise. Did Laon compromise his nonviolent tactics? And more important, does Shelley's view of nonviolence allow violent resistance in protection of "natural rights"? To Gandhi the answer to these questions is relative and is to be found in
the individual's response to circumstance. A resister must use violence if he loses faith in nonviolence; but he should recognize that
the failure was within himself, and not in nonviolence.[26] We will return to Shelley's view of this particular dilemma in a later chapter
when we discuss his poem "Men of England".

Gerald McNiece has written of the "rude pikes" passage:

---

[26] We might remember here that Gandhi actively supported England in
both the Boer War and World War I. He wrote: "I do believe that, where
there is only a choice between cowardice and violence, I would advise
violence" ("The Doctrine of the Sword", in *The Pacifist Conscience*, 217).
Shelley, of course, supported the Greek revolution, among others.

Laon fought, however, and shed blood when the enemy returned. Apparently Shelley did not think it inconsistent to distinguish between the way men may achieve the true society and what they must do when fighting for their lives, or perhaps fighting for their principles, since their lives were already given up, "As myriads flocked in love and brotherhood to die" (VI, 10). The time comes when passive resistance must end, and the law of necessity that ill will flow from ill loses its force of application.[27]

McNiece's interpretation is hasty, and, I believe, inaccurate. But John Guinn's response also presents problems. "Non-violent opposition even at the price of annihilation is the proper response to force of arms."[28] Generally speaking, Guinn's statement is valid concerning the presentation in *The Revolt of Islam* of the question of violence in human relationships. But it does not take into account the incident of the "rude pikes".

After careful examination of the text, I cannot conclude that Laon "shed blood". There is no evidence to support McNiece's interpretation on this point. However, Laon did participate in the Patriots' shout of joy on the discovery of the pikes. Are we to conclude that Laon supported the armed resistance of the Patriots? Perhaps the answer lies in separating the actions of Laon, the poet in the poem, from the vision of Shelley, the poet of the poem, as Shelley asked us to do in the "Preface".[29] As McNiece points out the lives of the Patriots are already lost when they discover the cache of rude pikes. When they react with hope that the weapons and the violent resistance that they represent may yet save them, we are given the final premonition by the author of their inevitable doom. The confrontation between violence and nonviolence has already been presented repeatedly within the structure of the poem, and in each case when violence has been used no victory has been won, and when nonviolence has been employed victory has gone to the nonviolent party. We might anticipate such a pattern to hold true in the incident of the rude pikes, and it does. Neither the tyrant nor the Patriots are victors.

[27]   *Shelley and the Revolutionary Idea,* 201.
[28]   *Shelley's Political Thought,* 87.
[29]   "I trust that the reader will carefully distinguish between those opinions which have a dramatic propriety in reference to the characters which they are designed to elucidate, and such as are properly my own."

Both remain slaves, and as a consequence of their violent struggle are ravaged by pestilence and famine. Regrettably, Laon's precise actions during this episode are not clear, nor is Shelley's opinion of them. But one valid interpretation, it seems to me, is that Laon did not and would not stab anyone (especially since he has recently in a similar situation refused to do so [ll. 1790-1800]), but that he did and would encourage men to violently defend their right to existence, if violence were the only honorable way that they could conceive to do so. To some pacifists, such a policy may seem evasive and undesirable. We might point out, however, that Gandhi's response to such a situation was similar to Shelley's. "Injustice must be resisted. . . . No doubt the non-violent way is always the best, but where that does not come naturally the violent way is both necessary and honorable. Inaction here is rank cowardice and unmanly. It must be shunned at all cost."[30]

This incident in the poem, when in a time of extreme crisis the nonviolent Patriots turn to violence, is a dramatization of Shelley's belief that a change of governments is not the solution to world turmoil. The revolution must occur within the individual, not within his arbitrary institutions. The incident of the counter-revolution is also a tribute to Shelley's historical realism. The implication is that even if the French Revolution had been non-violent, even if the Patriots had remained nonviolent to the end, failure in terms of immediate, practical, temporal goals would have resulted. Austria, Russia, and perhaps even England, afraid of the democratic ideas which the revolution represented, would have eagerly conspired to suppress it. What then would lead Shelley to denounce the tactics of the French Revolution and to declare his nonviolent revolution the *beau ideal,* when in the historical circumstance of the late eighteenth century he believed either one would have been a failure in terms of permanent results? Shelley believed that a nonviolent revolution would have moved people closer to an understanding of the *beau ideal* society and the means to achieve it. In most cases a revolution in the minds and hearts of individuals is not a quick happening. Such a revolution as Shelley depicts would have moved people closer to a superior

[30] *Gandhi On Non-Violence,* 39.

moral and political vision. Such a revolution would have made people aware of their moral and political power, a power antithetical to the corrupt and dehumanizing power of the establishment. They would have realized that in their failure was the hope of the future.[31]

But the French Revolution was not nonviolent. Thus we have the primary motivation for Shelley's writing *The Revolt of Islam*. It was to produce through the magic of poetry an effect on the imaginations of people similar to the one a nonviolent French Revolution would have produced – to depict the courage and the grandeur involved in returning good for evil, to describe the potential for political reform inherent in nonviolent action, and to communicate the metaphysical truth that the state of salvation and the means of salvation are one.

4

In Canto VII we learn of Cythna's life since the time she was separated from Laon. She has been made the slave of a tyrant who has raped her, and then imprisoned her in an underground cave. In her isolation Cythna has had fits of madness, similar to Laon's, and she has given birth to a daughter whom the tyrant has taken from her. While imprisoned she has learned the truth about suffering humankind's *spiritus mundi,* as Laon has similarly done.

> "My mind became the book through which I grew
>   Wise in all human wisdom, and its cave,
> Which like a mine I rifled through and through,
>   To me the keeping of its secrets gave —
>   One mind, the type of all, the moveless wave
> Whose calm reflects all moving things that are,

[31] "It is the pacifist's obligation to be both realist and idealist; to face existing facts while never losing sight of the world which he desires to create. His part, as a living leaven within the lump of popular traditions and assumptions, may seem trivial in itself, yet his task is nothing less than an attempt to change the thinking of his nation, and beyond that of a greater society . . . . Our task is that of trying to change the course of history by acting as a revolutionary leaven within society" (Vera Brittain, "The Function of a Minority", in *The Pacifist Conscience*, 283-90).

Necessity, and love, and life, the grave,
And sympathy, fountains of hope and fear;
Justice, and truth, and time, and the world's natural sphere!"
(ll. 3100–8)

It might be illuminating to elucidate the significance of the ty-
rant-Cythna-Laon triangle by comparing it with a similarly developed plot in William Blake's *Visions of the Daughters of Albion*.[32] In this poem, first published in 1793, Blake explores the
man-woman relationship as it exists in a patriarchal, morally orthodox society, whose self-righteousness is based on a clear distinction between good and evil, enforced limitations on human
experience, and the agents of fear that blind the individual from
vision – superstition, hypocrisy, hatred, jealousy, and pride. The
central image of the poem is the familiar love triangle; Oothoon
is the central figure (a heroine similar to Cythna) caught between
the tyrannical, Urizen figure of Bromion, who authoritatively demands and at the same time selfishly exploits adherence to the established order, values, and traditions, and the egoistic figure of
Theotormon (a character who contrasts with Laon), who self-
righteously admires and at the same time selfishly refuses to recognize innocence, honesty, and love. Although Oothoon loves
Theotormon, and he "loves" her, Theotormon cannot forgive
Oothoon the fact that she was raped by Bromion. The major
focus of the poem, to borrow Damon's phrasing, is a series of la-
mentations in which Oothoon denounces the slavery of marriage,
secrecy, selfishness, and religious dogmas, and a series of hymns
in which she praises "the essential purity of love and the holiness
of sex".[33]

Blake posits the same morally bankrupt social and political
structure that Shelley does in *The Revolt of Islam*. Laon's and
Cythna's love for each other finds fruition where Theotormon's
and Oothoon's does not, because Laon imaginatively identifies
with Cythna, whereas Theotormon is blinded by the arbitrary
mores of self-interested kings and priests who equate sexual viola-

[32] *Blake: Complete Writings,* ed. Geoffrey Keynes (London: Oxford University Press, 1966).
[33] S. Foster Damon, *A Blake Dictionary* (New York: E. P. Dutton & Co.,
Inc., 1971), 308.

tion with a moral insufficiency in the victim. Laon is able to distinguish essential human truth from dogmatic utterances disguised as truth by a self-interested establishment, while Theotormon is not. To break with tradition demands revolutionary courage in the individual – the courage poetically glorified by both Blake and Shelley.[34]

We can perhaps briefly continue our analysis of the similarity in the ethical visions of Blake and Shelley. After Cythna is freed from her underwater cave by an earthquake, she is rescued by sailors. Once on board ship, she gives the sailors a lecture, the truth of which they recognize immediately.

> "To feel the peace of self-contentment's lot,
>   To own all sympathies, and outrage none,
> And in the inmost bowers of sense and thought,
>   Until life's sunny day is quite gone down,
>   To sit and smile with Joy, or, not alone,
> To kiss salt tears from the worn cheek of Woe;
>   To live, as if to love and live were one, —
> This is not faith or law, nor those who bow
> To thrones on Heaven or Earth, such destiny many know.
>
> "But children near their parents tremble now,
>   Because they must obey — one rules another,
> And as one Power rules both high and low,
>   So man is made the captive of his brother,
>   And Hate is throned on high with Fear her mother,
> Above the Highest — and those fountain-cells,
>   Whence love yet flowed when faith had choked all other,
> Are darkened — Woman as the bond-slave dwells
> Of man, a slave; and life is poisoned in its wells."

(ll. 3298–3315)

The message that Cythna didactically preaches is the same that Blake imaginatively dramatizes in the earliest of his minor prophecies, *Tiriel*. In this poem Blake explores family relationships as they exist in a society committed to authoritarian, dogmatic principles enforced by selfish, tyrannical power, and his conclusions

---

[34] For a brief discussion of Blake and nonviolence see John Sutherland's article "William Blake and Nonviolence", *The Nation* (April 29, 1969), 542-44. "The poet William Blake wrestled all his life with a very modern dilemma: how to be true to both revolutionary and nonviolent ideals" (542).

are similar to Cythna's. The parent-child relationship in such a society is based on trembling and dissembling: fear is used as a weapon to restrict the natural inclinations of the young and to command unquestioning obedience, and dishonesty is employed to perpetuate a self-deluding stance of moral righteousness and to foster a feeling of egocentric self-importance. The parent-child and the husband-wife relationships are thus analogous to the tyrant-citizen relationship of the larger paternal society: it is the relationship of slave-owner and slave. Tiriel, the tyrant king and father, fuses the two central figures of an authoritarian-structured society into a single image, and we witness the relationships between him and his parents, between him and his wife, between him and his children, between him and his brother, and between him and his subjects. The similar pattern of these respective relationships creates a cyclical texture, which reinforces the poem's major theme: fear begets fear. Tiriel, like Othman in *The Revolt of Islam*, "is a man who has spent his entire life trying to domineer over others and establish a reign of terror founded on moral virtue".[35]

Both Blake's and Shelley's purpose in writing poetry was to inspire the hearts, minds, and imaginations of men to break the cycle of human relationships based on restriction, fear, and violence, and to portray the promise of freedom, love, and nonviolence that beckons man to that Utopian state which Blake called "Jerusalem", and which Shelley called "Everlasting Spring". They propose to send the Comet of evil crashing from its pinnacle of power, and to restore the Morning Star of love to its rightful place in the existence of men.[36]

[35] Northrop Frye, *Fearful Symmetry* (Princeton: Princeton University Press, 1947), 242.
[36] Concerning an ideal society, Reiter says in connection with *The Revolt of Islam*: "Some say that it is not realistic to think that the world can be shaped ideally, that Shelley was incompetent to measure books by experience. They must also deny a moral world governed by love, for such a world is counter to all experience, and in this poem 'Love is celebrated as the sole law which should govern the moral world' (Preface). Yet they accept, ostensibly, a Christian civilization, and so they must either be described as schizophrenic or be accused of plain hypocrisy. Much better is it, in any case, to measure experience by books, the 'precious life-blood of a

Cythna's contagious message of hope and love is not only presented to the sailors through her didactic speech, but is also presented to the reader through dramatic irony. Cythna discovers that these sailors, even as she talks to them, are employed in transporting young maidens into slavery at the tyrant's palace. These men are kinsmen to the sailors that have carried her into slavery, thereby causing all her suffering and sorrow. But there is no hatred or revenge in her heart – for she lives by the new law. The sailors listen to her, and set the maidens free.

In the last four cantos the poem draws rapidly to a conclusion. Othman demands revenge, and his henchmen, the judges and priests, enthusiastically and moralistically fulfill his will. In some of the most vivid passages ever composed describing the aftermatch of war, the reader is imaginatively presented with the horror and futility of armed conflict. Plague, Famine, Pestilence, and Slaughter rule the land.

> It was not hunger now, but thirst. Each well
>   Was choked with rotting corpses, and became
> A cauldron of green mist made visible
>   At sunrise. Thither still the myriads come,
>   Seeking to quench the agony of the flame,
> Which raged like poison through their bursting veins;
>   Naked they were from torture, without shame,
> Spotted with nameless scars and lurid blains,
> Childhood, and youth, and age, writhing in savage pains.
>
> (ll. 3975–81)

Cannibalism becomes an accepted and necessary practice.

> There was no corn — in the wide market-place
>   All loathliest things, even human flesh, was sold;
> They weighed it in small scales — and many a face
>   Was fixed in eager horror then.
>
> (ll. 3955–8)

Such a situation is pointedly contrasted with the short-lived period that the Patriots were in power.

In the palace the king with his guards and priests "rioted in festival the while" (l. 4001), for they are untouched by the onslaught

---

master spirit,' than the other way around – realists notwithstanding, the Romantic vision is the world's only hope" (48).

of Famine. However, soon the dark shadow of Plague covers all.
Then the rich and the powerful join their anguished voices to
those of the impoverished. And as frequently happens in times of
national calamity, the people fall to fighting among themselves. But
one sly and sinister man, an Iberian priest (a "Christian priest"
in the original), is able to reunite the frightened people with a
prayer of cruelty and revenge – he turns their anger and frustration away from themselves and onto those whom he claims God
hates the most – Laon and Cythna and the freedom fighters.[37]
The priest says that God would be appeased only by human sacrifice, and he sets his fellow priests about enraging the ignorant populace.

> And Priests rushed through their ranks, some counterfeiting
>   The rage they did inspire, some mad indeed
> With their own lies; they said their god was waiting
>   To see his enemies writhe, and burn, and bleed, —
>   And that, till then, the snakes of Hell had need
> Of human souls: — three hundred furnaces
>   Soon blazed through the wide City, where, with speed,
> Men brought their infidel kindred to appease
> God's wrath, and while they burned, knelt round on quivering knees.
>
>   (ll. 4189–97)

Such a vision provokes thoughts of the terrors of Nazi Germany
in mid-twentieth century readers. Even after the evidence was in,
many people were not able to comprehend what happened at
Auschwitz and Dachau. But Shelley a "dreamer" who envisioned
man's unlimited capacity for good, also realized man's unlimited
potential for evil. Shelley knew what fear and superstition could

---

[37] Indictments of organized religion similar to Shelley's have been voiced
many times. For example, C. Wright Mills, "A Pagan Sermon to the Christian Clergy", in *The Pacifist Conscience*, 411-20. "World War III is already
so total that most of its causes are accepted as 'necessity'; most of its
meaning as 'realism.' In our world 'necessity' and 'realism' have become
ways to hide lack of moral imagination . . . . One reason for this lack, I am
going to argue, is what surely must be called the moral default of the
Christians . . . . By moral insensibility I refer to the mute acceptance – or
even the unawareness – of moral atrocity. I mean the lack of indignation
when confronted with moral horror. I mean the turning of this atrocity and
this horror into morally approved conventions of feeling" (412).

make men do. Man's inhumanity to man is the main obstacle to
Godhead.

The fires are lit and the Patriots courageously come forward
to willingly suffer martyrdom in the name of freedom – for they
have reached the vision of truth and their spirits are free from
fear.

> And, one by one, that night, young maidens came,
>   Beauteous and calm, like shapes of living stone
> Clothed in the light of dreams, and by the flame
>   Which shrank as overgorged, they laid them down,
>   And sung a low sweet song, of which alone
> One word was heard, and that was Liberty;
>   And that some kissed their marble feet, with moan
> Like love, and died; and then that they did die
> With happy smiles, which sunk in white tranquillity.

(ll. 4216–24)

Meanwhile the hunt for Laon and Cythna continues throughout
the kingdom. The king has put a bounty on their heads: he who
brings them in dead will be "the kingdom's heir", and he who
brings them in alive will marry the princess and "reign an equal
king" (l. 4161). The juxtaposition of fairy-tale motifs with the
horrors of persecution creates the effect of black humor; it creates
uneasy laughter about the all too easy folly of a creature that
can be motivated in the midst of famine and plague by the hope
of power and wealth.

Laon, who has slipped away from Cythna, disguises himself
and appears before the king. The priests and warriors are amazed
at his "gentle" manner and speech, which comes "as from a
heart/Void of all hate or terror" (ll. 4346-7).

> "Ye Princes of the Earth, ye sit aghast
>   Amid the ruin which yourselves have made,
> Yes, Desolation heard your trumpet's blast,
>   And sprang from sleep! — dark Terror has obeyed
>   Your bidding — O, that I whom ye have made
> Your foe, could set my dearest enemy free
>   From pain and fear! but evil casts a shade,
> Which cannot pass so soon, and Hate must be
> The nurse and parent still of an ill progeny."

(ll. 4351–9)

Laon has devoted his life to the nonviolent goal of bringing all men, masters and slaves, to the Promised Land. His purpose cannot be accomplished within his lifetime, but the meaning of his existence has been defined by Cythna's cry: "Thoughts have gone forth whose powers can sleep no more" (l. 2260).

Laon negotiates a deal whereby he will present himself to the tyrant in exchange for Cythna's safe passage to America. The tyrant agrees and Laon reveals his true identity. However, as the pyre is being readied, Cythna arrives on her "gigantic steed", and demands to be bound beside Laon. The king's oath is broken when the Iberian priest convinces Othman that it is God's will that Cythna be burned to death also. So Laon and Cythna are burned to death, and the tyrant's child through an emphatic experience expires with them. Then Laon and Cythna, now reunited with her child, sail out of time and space into the Temple of Immortality to take their place beside the other great contributors to mankind's search for freedom and justice.

Shelley called *The Revolt of Islam* his "first serious appeal to the Public" (Preface). As we have seen, at the dramatic center of the poem occurs a nonviolent revolution. In the first part of the poem we witness Laon and Cythna struggling against oppression – at first violently when Laon fails in his attempt to free the captured Cythna with violence and bloodshed, and then nonviolently when Laon and Cythna succeed in their attempt to free the people from the evil and oppression of the tyrant's rule. The second half of the poem deals with the violent and brutal intervention by foreign arms in behalf of the tyrant, the murder of the Patriots, the return to power of Othman and the consequences that result – violence, famine, plague, hatred, and superstition. Laon and Cythna are executed not because the nonviolent revolution failed, but because world circumstances were not ripe for its permanent establishment. Foreign despots conspire to defeat the new reign of peace and love shortly after it wins the acceptance of the people of Argolis. Through Shelley's artful use of the dream-convention and his philosophical belief in the collective unconscious, he is able to dramatize the infusion of Intellectual Beauty into the poet in the poem, which makes the earth-bound poet able to assimilate the meaning of Laon's and Cythna's thoughts and experiences, and thus communicate them to men. The resolution of the poem brings a realization of the power of Necessity, the potential for good inherent in the human will, and the hope that the forces of universal love will eventually succeed.[38]

Because Shelley realized that the time and circumstance denied his ascending to the role of hero-activist which he had desired in Ireland, he wrote *The Revolt of Islam* as an imaginative contribution to the nonviolent movement for reform which he envisioned developing strength after his death. Indeed, at this time his health was poor and he believed that death was imminent. "I felt the precariousness of my life, & I engaged in this task resolved to leave some record of myself. Much of what the volume contains was written with the same feeling, as real, though not so prophetic, as the communications of a dying man" (432). Yet even before *The Revolt* was published Shelley was contemplating another work "which a serious & earnest estimate of my powers will suggest to me, & which will be in every respect accommodated to their utmost limits" (432).[39] While Shelley defended his effort in *The Revolt* against Godwin's criticism, and claimed "that it was in many respects a genuine picture of my own mind" (432), he knew that his poem was not without faults. In the "Preface" he considers whether the poem's flaws irreparably doom it to oblivion:

Should the Public judge that my composition is worthless, I shall indeed bow before the tribunal from which Milton received his crown of immortality; and shall seek to gather, if I live, strength from that defeat, which may nerve me to some new enterprise of thought which may *not* be worthless.

The Revolt of Islam failed to arouse any public interest in Shel-

---

[38] "Even in the utmost apparent defeat, love is victorious; hope is created out of the wreck of hope. That is the eternal truth behind the symbol of the Cross; and this is the truth Shelley is proclaiming". F. A. Lea, *Shelley and the Romantic Revolution* (1905; rpt. Folcroft, Pa.: Folcroft Press, Inc., 1969), 103.

[39] Also compare Shelley's "Dedication, To Mary":
Is it, that now my inexperienced fingers
  But strike the prelude of a loftier strain?
Or, must the lyre on which my spirit lingers
  Soon pause in silence, ne'er to sound again? (ll. 82-5)

ley's lifetime, and has aroused very little since.[40] But it does have its place not only in the context of Shelley's poetic and philosophical development, but as an ambitious and often successful epic that pleads for the necessity of nonviolence in human relationships. But as Shelley prepared to leave England for Italy, the poem that was then germinating in his creative imagination, *Prometheus Unbound*, was to succeed where *The Revolt of Islam* had failed. It would be a lyrical dramatization on the theme of nonviolence that had inspired *The Revolt*, but it would be a sustained poetic effort that would test Shelley's powers at their limits.

[40] Stovall, *Desire and Restraint in Shelley*, 160.

V

PROMETHEUS UNBOUND

> But vain the Sword & vain the Bow
> They never can work War's overthrow.
> The Hermit's Prayer and the Widow's tear
> Alone can free the World from fear.
>
> For a Tear is an Intellectual Thing,
> And a Sigh is the Sword of an Angel King,
> And the bitter groan of the Martyr's woe
> Is an Arrow from the Almightie's Bow.
>
> William Blake, "The Grey Monk"
>
> There is no way to peace. Peace is the way.
>
> A. J. Muste

Prometheus Unbound was composed in Italy in a period of a little over a year. The first act was written at Este in the fall of 1818,
the second and third acts at Rome during March and April,
1919, and the fourth act at Florence during the late fall of 1919.
Shelley's life in exile was not a happy one, especially during the
time when he was composing *Prometheus Unbound*. The family
moved frequently in search of climate that might improve Shelley's ailing health. The two children of Mary and Shelley, Clara
and William, died during this time.[1] Mary was despondent, and
Shelley far from England felt alienated and alone in what at times
must have seemed to him to be a hostile universe.[2] Yet it was during
this time that he fulfilled his promise to Godwin. *Prometheus Unbound* did accommodate Shelley's powers "to their utmost limits" (432). And despite the personal hardships of his life during

---

[1] White, *Shelley*, Chapters XX-XXII.

[2] In a letter to Peacock, June, 1819, Shelley wrote: "O that I could return
to England! How heavy a weight when misfortune is added to exile, and
solitude, as if the measure were not full, heaped high on both – O that I
could return to England!" (501).

this period, the poem is a magnificent and full statement of Shelley's optimistic belief in man's potential to fulfill his humanity through suffering and love.

In *The Revolt of Islam* Shelley retold the story of the French Revolution in a way designed to appeal to the moral imaginations of men. In *Prometheus Unbound* his purpose is similar. He reinterprets the myth of Prometheus as written by Aeschylus in a way designed, as he declares in the "Preface", to appeal to the empathic imaginations "of the more select classes of poetical readers" (II, 174).[3] In Aeschylus' lost play, Prometheus through self-interest and through fear of pain capitulates to Jupiter and compromises his integrity. In Shelley's poem, as we might expect, there is no self-interested compromise with tyranny. Shelley writes in the "Preface" to the poem:

The *Prometheus Unbound* of Aeschylus supposed the reconciliation of Jupiter with his victim as the price of the danger threatened to his empire by the consummation of his marriage with Thetis. Thetis, according to this view of the subject, was given in marriage to Peleus, and Prometheus, by the permission of Jupiter, delivered from his captivity by Hercules. Had I framed my story on this model, I should have done no more than have attempted to restore the lost drama of Aeschylus; . . . But, in truth, I was averse from a catastrophe so feeble as that of reconciling the Champion with the Oppressor of mankind. The moral interest of the fable, which is so powerfully sustained by the sufferings and endurance of Prometheus, would be annihilated if we could conceive of him unsaying his high language and quailing before his successful and perfidious adversary. . . . But Prometheus is, as it were, the type of the highest perfection of moral and intellectual nature, impelled by the purest and the truest motives to the best and noblest ends (II, 171–2).

The theme of *Prometheus Unbound* is basically the same as the theme of *The Revolt of Islam*.[4] At the dramatic center of the lyri-

---

[3]   Shelley wrote to Ollier, March 6, 1820: " 'Prometheus Unbound,' I must tell you, is my favourite poem; I charge you, therefore, specially to pet him and feed him with fine ink and good paper . . . . I think, if I may judge by its merits, the 'Prometheus' cannot sell beyond twenty copies" (551).
[4]   McNiece gives a helpful comparative analysis of *The Revolt of Islam* and *Prometheus Unbound*, 216-7. "*Prometheus Unbound* re-enacts the events of *The Revolt of Islam*. The basic plot is the same. Separated powers in human nature are reunited, and from their union arises the sense of a

cal drama is a successful nonviolent revolution.[5] As long as Prometheus accepts the efficacy of revenge and violence as legitimate modes of human behavior, he remains chained to the rock – a rock that represents his own limitations (Laon, we recall, was similarly chained). But when Prometheus realizes the power of will, of love, of truth, of suffering, or self-purification, and of forgiveness, he is able to free himself, and symbolically all mankind, from Jupiter's tyrannical oppression, and thereby to give to man the gifts of freedom and justice. When Prometheus, who on one level of symbolic interpretation is the ultimate imaginative potential of collective man, embraces Asia, who is a symbol of pure, eternal love, then fear and violence are removed from man's universe. Prometheus is mythically the deliverer of mankind and symbolically the collective potential of mankind artistically fused into a single image of the Promethean fire-gift divinizing the human will – man becoming God.

When we compare *Prometheus Unbound* with "An Address to the Irish People" and *The Revolt of Islam,* we notice that Shelley has shifted the focus of his subject matter. Shelley's greatest work concerns itself with the revolution of the human spirit rather than the reform of society in general. But the shift in emphasis does not mean a change in philosophy. In the "Address" Shelley maintained that there must be a reform of the individual before society as a whole could be reformed. But both processes go on simultaneously in time. Perfection of the individual need not be accomplished before reform of society begins. That is why Shelley could be composing Act IV of *Prometheus Unbound* and "A Philosophical View of Reform" at roughly the same time. The latter work proposes specific, practical, gradual means of reform for the English society of 1819; the former work dramatizes the permanent and spiritual means of transformation for all men

new and enriched and beautiful world which acts on human hopes as a guiding beacon" (216).
[5] Earl Wasserman says in his analysis of the poem: "Shelley will not admit that the effective revolutionary overthrow of evil and tyranny can be a violent, hatefilled destruction: violence begets only the means of further violence" (*Shelley's Prometheus Unbound* [Baltimore: Johns Hopkins Press, 1965], 113).

in all ages. Thus we, too, in this chapter will shift the emphasis of our investigation. We will analyze Shelley's nonviolent philosophy as it applies to the individual in his attempt at self-purification – that is, the elimination of fear and the products of fear, violence and hatred, from self, and the infusion of love and the products of love, truth and justice, in self. We will attempt to comprehend Shelley's metaphysics of nonviolence – his religion of love. Perhaps now we can begin our analysis of the poem in an attempt to see Shelley's expression of nonviolence not simply as a political force for reform, but as a meaningful way of life.

1

As Act I opens, Prometheus is discovered chained to the precipice of icy rocks. As he speaks morning slowly breaks.

> Monarch of Gods and Daemons, and all Spirits
> But One, who throng those bright and rolling worlds
> Which Thou and I alone of living things
> Behold with sleepless eyes! regard this Earth
> Made multitudinous with thy slaves, whom thou
> Requitest for knee-worship, prayer, and praise,
> And toil, and hecatombs of broken hearts,
> With fear and self-contempt and barren hope.
> Whilst me, who am thy foe, eyeless in hate,
> Hast thou made reign and triumph, to thy scorn,
> O'er mine own misery and thy vain revenge.
> Three thousand years of sleep-unsheltered hours,
> And moments aye divided by keen pangs
> Till they seemed years, torture and solitude,
> Scorn and despair, — these are mine empire.
> More glorious far than that which thou surveyest
> From thine unenvied throne, O, Mighty God!
> Almighty, had I deigned to share the shame
> Of thine ill tyranny, and hung not here
> Nailed to this wall of eagle-baffling mountain.   (I, 1–20)

In Prometheus' opening speech we are given a brief glimpse of his dark night of the soul. He has been tortured physically and mentally for three thousand years by Jupiter – a Blakean Urizenic figure who on the political level represents the tyranny of kings and priests, and on the psychic level represents the evil impulses within Prometheus himself. For while Prometheus is the hope of mankind because he refuses to submit to Jupiter's rule, he also chains himself to pain and inaction through his hate of the tyrant and his desire for revenge.[6] The intensity of his suffering has produced profound spiritual anguish and egocentric self-pity and brought Prometheus to the edge of despair. In this state he speaks the words which give him a new commitment to life, and his spiritual state immediately begins to change. Thus the climax of the play occurs within the first sixty lines.

> And yet to me welcome is day and night,
> Whether one breaks the hoar frost of the morn,
> Or starry, dim, and slow, the other climbs
> The leaden-coloured east; for then they lead
> The wingless, crawling hours, one among whom
> — As some dark Priest hales the reluctant victim —
> Shall drag thee, cruel King, to kiss the blood
> From these pale feet, which then might trample thee
> If they disdained not such a prostrate slave.
> Disdain! Ah no! I pity thee. What ruin
> Will hunt thee undefended through wide Heaven!
> How will thy soul, cloven to its depth with terror,
> Gape like a hell within! I speak in grief,
> Not exultation, for I hate no more,
> As then ere misery made me wise. The curse
> Once breathed on thee I would recall.   (I, 44–59)

– "for I hate no more". Through his suffering ("ere misery made me wise") Prometheus has gained the knowledge that evil is its own worst enemy. To exist with hate and revenge in his heart toward Jupiter is to reduce his spirit to the level of Jupiter's, and thus to be a partner in evil. It is to chain his soul to the forces of death and destruction. His realization that this is what he himself has done, leads him to sympathize with the unwitting position of Jupiter – and to pity him. His imagination through an empathic

---

[6] "The power of Jupiter comes from Prometheus' acknowledging Jupiter as an existent negation, and then wishing pain and destruction upon that negation. To hate and reject so intensely is to become that which one hates. By deciding that Jupiter is a contrary force to be transcended, Prometheus achieves a dialectic of release" (Harold Bloom, *The Visionary Company* [Garden City: Doubleday & Company, Inc., 1961], 323).

experience brings his will to act. Prometheus asks that the curse he gave to Jupiter be recalled, so that comprehending the desire for revenge he once had, he may revoke it. He is answered by four spirit-songs of the natural world who have had such havoc wreaked on their existence because of the curse that they dare not repeat it. The Earth spirit says that so much "misery" has resulted that none dare mention the curse. In issuing the curse Prometheus has defied the tyrant, but in his hatred of the tyrant he has given Jupiter the power to divide and destroy the natural world of man's existence.

Although Earth says that no living thing may utter the curse, she informs Prometheus that he may call a phantasm of the dead who can recite it. Prometheus, in the manner of Faustus, quickly demands that the phantasm of Jupiter appear and repeat the curse. The phantasm responds:

> Heap on thy soul, by virtue of this Curse,
>   Ill deeds, then be thou damned, beholding good;
> Both infinite as is the universe,
>   And thou, and thy self-torturing solitude.
> An awful image of calm power
> Though now thou sittest, let the hour
> Come, when thou must appear to be
>   That which thou art internally.
> And after many a false and fruitless crime
> Scorn track thy lagging fall thro' boundless space and time.
>
> (I, 292–301)

Prometheus' curse is that evil should be recognized as evil in the minds and hearts of men, and as a result of such recognition should fall from power in the world of space and time. This is exactly, of course, what happens in the play. Recognition of the evil within and without the mind of man is the primary step in eliminating its power over man. Prometheus realizes that revenge and hate are evils – no matter what good-will he who hates might intend. This realization portends Jupiter's downfall, and also provides hope that a similar tyrant will not replace him. When mankind imaginatively realizes that which is evil in existence, the "emblems" of evil's dominion in the world, stripped of their authoritarian and superstitious masks, will be "unregarded" by men and will topple of their own dead weight (III, iv, 164-89). When man recognizes evil he will refuse to cooperate with it – and his positive act of non-cooperation will cause evil to lose dominion in the world of men. Good and evil are as "infinite as the universe", and it is the will of man that gives evil the power to dominate. Prometheus expresses sorrow for his sin.

> It doth repent me: words are quick and vain;
> Grief for awhile is blind, and so was mine.
> I wish no living thing to suffer pain. (I, 303–5)

Prometheus' admission of his mistake and the forgiveness of his enemy are the reclamation of his humanity. His new found respect for life – "I wish no living thing to suffer pain" – is similar to William Blake's dictum – "Everything that lives is holy." Ironically, the spirit of Earth takes Prometheus' forgiveness of Jupiter as a sign of defeat.

> Misery, oh misery to me,
> That Jove at length should vanquish thee.
> Wail, howl aloud, Land and Sea,
> The Earth's rent heart shall answer ye.
> Howl, Spirits of the living and the dead,
> Your refuge, your defence lies fallen and vanquished. (I, 306–11)

The irony of the Earth's dirge to the "fallen and vanquished" hero at the moment of his most courageous and charitable act is obvious. It is much to the point that Shelley had made in *The Revolt of Islam* and elsewhere. The Earth represents all the well-meaning souls who through a lack of moral imagination confuse good with ill.

> The good want power, but to weep barren tears.
> The powerful goodness want: worse need for them.
> The wise want love; and those who love want wisdom;
> And all best things are thus confused to ill. (I, 625–8)

The Earth loves Prometheus as a mother, but she is not a very wise parent. She has been swayed by the divisive dictates of Jupiter and thus would unwittingly destroy and demean that which she loves. She admires Prometheus' proud defiance and hatred of the tyrant, and his promise of violent revenge; but she aban-

dons hope when Prometheus engages in humility and forgiveness
– as Judas once abandoned Christ, as the Weathermen abandoned the Students for a Democratic Society. Although she will
not remain so deceived, Earth has been brainwashed by Jupiter
into believing that violence is the proper response to violence, that
hate should answer hate. But as we have pointed out before,
Shelley understood that to play the game of life according to tyranny's rules is to spiritually sink to the bestial level of the oppressor, and pragmatically to fall into his hands – for violence and
repression are the games he understands best.

Ione and Panthea, spiritual sisters of Asia and her intuitive
link with Prometheus, although they do not understand the significance of the Titan's act, realize that he "is unvanquished still".
They announce the arrival of Mercury, messenger from Jupiter,
and the Furies from hell sent to increase Prometheus' torture and
suffering. Mercury speaks:

Awful Sufferer
To thee unwilling, most unwillingly
I come, by the great Father's will driven down,
To execute a doom of new revenge.
Alas! I pity thee, and hate myself
That I can do no more: aye from thy sight
Returning, for a season, Heaven seems Hell,
So thy worn form pursues me night and day,
Smiling reproach. Wise art thou, firm and good,
But vainly wouldst stand forth alone in strife
Against the Omnipotent; as yon clear lamps
That measure and divide the weary years
From which there is no refuge, long have taught
And long must teach. Even now thy Torturer arms
With the strange might of unimagined pains
The powers who scheme slow agonies in Hell,
And my commission is to lead them here,
Or what more subtle, foul, or savage fiends
People the abyss, and leave them to their task.   (I, 352–70)

As Shelley has drawn him, Mercury has more than a touch of
Shakespeare's Osric, the dandified, swift-talking messenger from
the powers-that-be. Indeed, it is interesting to see how Shelley
deviated from Aeschylus in making Mercury sympathetic rather

than unsympathetic to Prometheus. Mercury is a stereotype of another human attitude toward despotism and evil. If Earth is love without wisdom, Mercury is wisdom without love. He is wise in the ways of the world. In an attempt to escape pain and commitment he has sold out to Jupiter. He doesn't like being a messenger of evil, but it does have its advantages, its sense of security,[7] and it certainly is preferable, or so he thinks, to the suffering of the nonconformist, of Prometheus. Mercury's attitude is similar to the one held by citizens who participate in a war effort, either by carrying a gun, making munitions, or paying taxes, and who realize that the war they support is evil – a product of Shelley's Jupiter, or of Blake's Urizen. It is an attitude that holds that one person can't fight the system, that it is prudent to compromise integrity, support an evil system, and live a life of painless apathy, bothered only by occasional pricks of conscience – such as confronting the misery of Prometheus, or the horror of Mylai. Mercury's speech to Prometheus is like a pragmatist's to a pacifist. He advises Prometheus to submit to Jupiter's omnipotence and thus free himself from suffering. Prometheus replies:

> He who is evil can receive no good;
> And for a world bestowed, or a friend lost,
> He can feel hate, fear, shame; not gratitude:
> He but requites me for his own misdeed.
> Kindness to such is keen reproach, which breaks
> With bitter stings the light sleep of Revenge.
> Submission, thou dost know I cannot try;
> For what submission but that fatal word,
> The death-seal of mankind's captivity,
> Like the Sicilian's hair-suspended sword,
> Which trembles o'er his crown, would he accept,
> Or could I yield? Which yet I will not yield.
> Let others flatter Crime, where it sits throned
> In brief Omnipotence: secure are they:
> For Justice, when triumphant, will weep down
> Pity, not punishment, on her own wrongs,
> Too much avenged by those who err.   (I, 389–405)

[7] Bayard Rustin has put it thus: "nothing that is good, personal or social, can begin to occur so long as there is any effort to pursue security" (*Protest: Pacifism and Politics*, ed. James Finn [New York: Random House, 1968], 328).

Prometheus will not submit, nor will he be provoked again into despair, into a desire for revenge. He will return only kindness for hate. He will not "flatter crime" as Mercury does, for he now realizes that the endless cycle of returning evil for evil can be broken by an act of forgiveness. Do not pity me, says Prometheus, but "pity the self-despising slaves of heaven" – the Rosencrantzes and Guildensterns.

Mercury calls up the furies to torture Prometheus. They are the ministers "of pain, and fear, / And disappointment, and mistrust, and hate, / And clinging crime" (I, 452-4). The second fury says to Prometheus: "Dost imagine / We will but laugh into thy lidless eyes?" (I, 478-9). And Prometheus heroically replies: "I weigh not what ye do, but what ye suffer, / Being evil" (I, 480-1).

Prometheus now realizes that evil is its own worst enemy, its own punishment. He had suffered long and painfully for his hate of Jupiter, but now because his will has cast out hate, within his "mind sits peace serene" (I, 430). His moral imagination is now alert –

> Methinks I grow like what I contemplate,
> And laugh and stare in loathsome sympathy.
>
> (I, 450–1)

Prometheus can even be sympathetic to the mad furies – return pity for their hate – because he can imaginatively comprehend the unfortunate and misguided meaning of their existence. They are slaves of a slave. To sympathize with them is to understand what makes the furies mad and to pity their lamentable state. Where there is pity there is no fear, and without the element of fear the furies are powerless to subsume the human will.

The furies produce visions which are Prometheus' most severe tortures yet – and they are spiritual and psychological rather than physical. The first vision is the crucifixion of Christ.

> Hark that outcry of despair!
> 'Tis his mild and gentle ghost
>   Wailing for the faith he kindled.
>
> (I, 553–5)

The second is the French Revolution.

> The nations thronged around, and cried aloud,
> As with one voice, Truth, liberty, and love!
> Suddenly fierce confusion fell from heaven
> Among them: there was strife, deceit, and fear:
> Tyrants rushed in, and did divide the spoil.
> This was the shadow of the truth I saw.   (I, 650–5)

Prometheus is given historical visions which attempt to demonstrate the futility of his high purposes, the absurdity of his existence. He is given the agony of watching Christ crucified and nations butchered for attempting to do what Prometheus himself wishes to do – divorce the evil principle from himself and symbolically all humanity. These are but two of many cases in history in which the spirit of good has warred with the spirit of evil and been defeated, and after the defeat the good principles have been turned into repressive evils by the forces of Jupiter – as priests have done to the teachings of Christ – as emperors have done to the hopes of the French Revolution. Prometheus is being given a lesson in history. It is a lesson to which both Earth and Mercury have succumbed.

History is used by the furies of hell in an attempt to produce despair in Prometheus. It is used to quell his spirit and destroy his will. The lesson of history, of Christ and the French Revolution, is that evil and violence are a necessary condition of man from which he cannot escape. Thus history is one of the main psychological weapons of Jupiter. For Prometheus to free himself, for man to free himself, he must escape from history – he must extinguish the past – "Oh, might it die or rest at last."[8] According to Thomas Merton, such a belief was fundamental to the philosophy of Mahatma Gandhi as well.

The greatest of man's spiritual needs is the need to be delivered from the evil and falsity that are in himself and his society. Tyranny, which makes a sagacious use of every human need and indeed artificially creates more of them in order to exploit them all to the limit, recognizes the importance of guilt. And modern tyrannies have all explicitly or implicitly in one way or another emphasized the *irreversibility of evil* in order to build their power upon it.[9]

[8] As Woodring states, Shelley believed "the inherited sin is Malthusian despair of reform" (*Politics in English Romantic Poetry,* 310).
[9] "Introduction", *Gandhi On Non-Violence,* 11.

Prometheus refuses to be confined by history, and he breaks the cycle of evil that dooms men to despair, a despair they sometimes euphemistically call "realism". Would that contemporary world-leaders and the citizens that encourage them likewise could break the cycle of arms' races and protective bombings!

Act I ends when Earth sends a group of healing spirits – beholders of the future – to comfort Prometheus. Their lyric songs tell Prometheus that his courage has assured the continuance of love, revolution, wisdom, and poetry. They bring hope to Prometheus with their prophecy of the coming nonviolent revolution.

> Thou shalt quell this horseman grim,
> Woundless though in heart or limb. (I, 787–8)

Prometheus is comforted, but he realizes that without love all hope is futile.

> How fair these airborn shapes! and yet I feel
> Most vain all hope but love; and thou art far,
> Asia! (I, 807–9)

Panthea assures Prometheus that Asia is not as far away as he thinks, and that his act of forgiveness has already begun to thaw the "desolate and frozen" waste of her exile.

2

Act II opens in the Indian Caucasus with a soliloquy by Asia. She represents love, fertility, the promise of a new life. Because Prometheus has given up the hate which filled his being, his thoughts have now turned to Asia and the love they once shared. His hate has separated him from his most powerful ally – love. Asia intuitively realizes the change that has occurred within the soul of Prometheus, and her transformation begins immediately.

> There is a change: beyond their inmost depth
> I see a shade, a shape: 'tis He, arrayed
> In the soft light of his own smiles, which spread
> Like radiance from the cloud-surrounded moon.
> Prometheus, it is thine! depart not yet! (II, 119–23)

Asia, in the words of Harold Bloom, "must be born again" before she can be reunited with Prometheus.[10] Thus she begins a descent to the cave of Demogorgon to discover the time of her rebirth, of man's liberation, and of their reunion in wisdom and peace. The descent of Asia and Panthea to the underworld apparently is a movement away from the world of sensual and rational experience to a state of imaginative existence where reality is confronted, and where prophecy is sung in "those wise and lovely songs" –

> Of fate, and chance, and God, and Chaos old,
> And Love, and the chained Titan's woful doom,
> And how he shall be loosed, and make the earth
> One brotherhood.
>
> (II, ii, 91–5)

At the depth of her descent Asia reaches the cave of Demogorgon and confronts him with a series of questions about the meaning of life; but Demogorgon can tell her nothing more than what is already known to man. She asks him about the problem of evil in the world.

> And who made terror, madness, crime, remorse,
> Which from the links of the great chain of things,
> To every thought within the mind of man
> Sway and drag heavily, and each one reels
> Under the load towards the pit of death;
> Abandoned hope, and love that turns to hate;
> And self-contempt, bitterer to drink than blood;
> Pain, whose unheeded and familiar speech
> Is howling, and keen shrieks, day after day;
> And Hell, or the sharp fear of Hell?   (II, iv, 19–28)

Asia receives only the ambiguous answer "He reigns" from Demogorgon. But "He" is not the "Merciful God" (II, iv, 18) who is responsible for the Spirit of good in the world, but Jupiter, the Spirit of evil which presently reigns over the world of men. The origin of evil is not revealed to Asia because Demogorgon's "deep truth is imageless" (II, iv, 116), and not communicable to man.

[10] Bloom, *The Visionary Company*, 326.

> What to bid speak
> Fate, Time, Occasion, Chance, and Change? To these
> All things are subject but eternal Love.
>
> (II, iv, 118–20)

Good and evil war within the human spirit eternally, and love is the only means by which man can assure the perpetual triumph of good over evil. As Asia enters the chariot of the Spirit of the Hour to make her return journey, she learns of Jupiter's impending doom and her reunion with Prometheus – the hour of revolution is at hand. As Asia travels toward Prometheus her transformation is completed. Panthea speaks:

> How thou art changed! I dare not look on thee;
> I feel but see thee not. I scarce endure
> The radiance of thy beauty. Some good change
> Is working in the elements, which suffer
> Thy presence thus unveiled.
> . . . .
>   love, like the atmosphere
> Of the sun's fire filling the living world,
> Burst from thee, and illumined earth and heaven
> And the deep ocean and the sunless caves
> And all that dwells within them; till grief cast
> Eclipse upon the soul from which it came:
> Such art thou now; nor is it I alone,
> Thy sister, thy companion, thine own chosen one,
> But the whole world which seeks thy sympathy.
> Hearest thou not sounds i' the air which speak the love
> Of all articulate beings?
>
> (II, v, 16-20, 26-36)

This is one of many passages in the poem in which Shelley's recent, intensive study of Plato can be seen.[11] Love is being transformed into something so beautiful that the world consciously prefers it to evil. It is becoming so beautiful that it is recognized as the obvious good. Act II closes with a song by Asia celebrating her rebirth – an experience she articulates as a movement from old age backwards to infancy and then into a state of existence beyond time where love is fully realized.

---

[11] For the influence of Plato on Shelley, particularly in *Prometheus Unbound,* consult Grabo, Chapters XI-XIII.

> We have passed Age's icy caves,
>   And Manhood's dark and tossing waves,
> And Youth's smooth ocean, smiling to betray:
>   Beyond the glassy gulfs we flee
>   Of shadow-peopled Infancy,
> Through Death and Birth, to a diviner day.   (II, v, 98–104)

We might emphasize again that Asia's transformation has only been possible because of her intuitive response to Prometheus' act of will – his expulsion of hate and desire for love.

Act III opens in heaven with Jupiter on his throne. In Jupiter's opening speech we are dramatically presented with his pride and egoism, and through dramatic irony we are presented with an oppressor as enslaved as those he oppresses, enslaved to the hysteria of his hate and to his desire for increased power. In his own way Jupiter suffers as he has made Prometheus suffer – he suffers the pains of jealousy because the will of Prometheus refuses to yield.

> Ye congregated powers of heaven, who share
> The glory and the strength of him ye serve,
> Rejoice! henceforth I am omnipotent.
> All else had been subdued to me; alone
> The soul of man, like unextinguished fire,
> Yet burns towards heaven with fierce reproach, and doubt,
> And lamentation, and reluctant prayer,
> Hurling up insurrection, which might make
> Our antique empire insecure, though built
> On eldest faith, and hell's coeval, fear.
> . . . .
> It [soul of man] yet remains supreme o'er misery,
> Aspiring, unrepressed, yet soon to fall;
> Even now have I begotten a strange wonder,
> That fatal child, the terror of the earth,
> Who waits but till the destined hour arrive,
> Bearing from Demogorgon's vacant throne
> The dreadful might of ever-living limbs
> Which clothed that awful spirit unbeheld,
> To redescend, and trample out the spark.
>
>   (III, i, 1–10, 16–24)

Jupiter is seen at his proudest moment, on the verge (so he thinks) of total victory over persistent enemy – Prometheus. But Jupiter is wrong in his belief that his union with Thetis will produce a "fatal child" capable of destroying and conquering the will of man. At the pinnacle of Jupiter's fiendish ecstasy Demogorgon arrives. "What art thou?" demands Jupiter.

> Eternity. Demand no direr name.
> Descend, and follow me down the abyss.
> I am thy child, as thou wert Saturn's child;
> Mightier than thee: and we must dwell together
> Henceforth in darkness. Lift thy lightnings not.
>
> (III, i, 52–6)

Demogorgon is not the child that Jupiter has expected. But he is Jupiter's progeny in the sense that "despotism sows the seeds of its own decay and will inevitably, in spite of its own efforts to survive, be banished from the earth".[12] Jupiter pleads:

> Detested prodigy!
> Even thus beneath the deep Titanian prisons
> I trample thee! thou lingerest?
>   Mercy! mercy!
> No pity, no release, no respite! Oh,
> That thou wouldst make mine enemy my judge,
> Even where he hangs, seared by my long revenge,
> Oh Caucasus! he would not doom me thus.
> Gentle, and just, and dreadless, is he not
> The monarch of the world? What then art thou?
> No refuge! no appeal!
>
> (III, i, 61–9)

Demogorgon is the law of inevitability – Necessity. Jupiter cannot crush Demogorgon beneath his feet as he once attempted to crush all else. Prometheus likewise cannot grant a reprieve to tyranny because evil necessarily must be subsumed by time and the will of man. But another tyranny will replace the one deposed by Demogorgon unless Prometheus, the collective imaginative potential of man, becomes united with Asia, unchanging love, and together they perpetually renew their dedication to life. Prometheus tells Asia of the everlasting spring that awaits them.

---

[12] Kenneth Neill Cameron, "The Political Symbolism of *Prometheus Unbound*", 751.

The gathered rays which are reality,
Shall visit us, the progeny immortal
Of Painting, Sculpture, and rapt Poesy,
And arts, though unimagined, yet to be.
The wandering voices and the shadows these
Of all that man becomes, the mediators
Of that best worship love, by him and us
Given and returned; swift shapes and sounds, which grow
More fair and soft as man grows wise and kind,
And veil by veil, evil and error fall:
Such virtue has the cave and place around.

(III, iii, 53–63)

The union of Prometheus and Asia is the union of wisdom and love, of man and nature, of man and woman, of psyche and epipsyche. Their union assures the rule of the spirit of good in a world of time and change. Asia, like Cythna before her, is the agent of love in revolution – that which keeps a revolution from producing violence, fanaticism, and fascism.[13] As long as love exists in the mind and heart of man, evil produced by fear and hatred will be subsumed. But man must continuously and actively work to attain and maintain such a state of existence. Shelley's apocalypse, like Blake's, is a state of energy and action, not of stasis and immutability.[14] Man must continue to perform physical, mental, and spiritual acts that will increase his imaginative awareness of existence. Inaction produces decay of these various faculties which will lead to a resurgence of evil in the world.[15] In the state of Utopia man is in a constant state of building Utopia, a state of becoming, a state of ecstasy. Shelley makes it clear ("as man grows wise and kind") that at the advent of the revolution of love man will not immediately attain a state of static perfection and

[13] McNiece, p. 233.
[14] "Like Blake, Shelley refuses to visualize a static heaven, an upper paradise without change, choice, danger, and the naturalistic completion of death. There is no mysterious invisible in Shelley's vision of last things; death survives, but so do we, by mastering death without ending it and replacing the religion of the remote sky with a renewed earth" (Bloom, *The Visionary Company*, 333).
[15] Mrs. Shelley erred when she wrote in her "Note on *Prometheus Unbound*", that Shelley believed "that evil is not inherent in the system of the creation, but an accident that might be expelled" (See White, *Shelley*, II, 123).

thereby negate the energy that is his humanity. For man will remain man – he will not become some sort of disinterested angel.

> The painted veil, by those who were, called life,
> Which mimicked, as with colours idely spread,
> All men believed or hoped, is torn aside;
> The loathsome mask has fallen, the Man remains, —
> Sceptreless, free, uncircumscribed, — but man:
> Equal, unclassed, tribeless and nationless,
> Exempt from awe, worship, degree, — the King
> Over himself; just, gentle, wise, — but man:
> Passionless? no: yet free from guilt or pain,
> Which were, for his will made, or suffered them,
> Nor yet exempt, though ruling them like slaves,
> From chance, and death, and mutability,
> The clogs of that which else might oversoar
> The loftiest star of unascended heaven,
> Pinnacled dim in the intense inane.   (III, iv, 190–204)

Jupiter's empire has fallen of necessity; the loathsome masks of his power have been torn away; thrones and altars, "the pride of kings and priests", stand unregarded; the emblems that men once served with blood and death no longer blind and enslave them; Prometheus' act of forgiveness and his subsequent union with suffering love, Asia, is a new beginning. At the conclusion of Act III Prometheus stands before us an example of regenerate man as Shelley envisioned him – a symbol of man's potential realized.

By the conclusion of Act III Shelley has created his myth. Act IV is a lyrical hymn to regenerate man and a musical celebration of life. As Bloom states, "the poem becomes its own subject matter".[16] Prometheus and Asia are not dramatically present in the final act, an act which is a "nuptial song" to their passionate physical and spiritual reunion.[17] Act IV is a celebration of the human spirit and the glory in which it could exist; it is not an attempt to depict the best of all possible worlds, but rather it is an attempt to promote the belief that a better world is possible.[18]

Structurally we can divide the final act into three thematic movements, although such a distinction is arbitrary since the final act

16   Bloom, *The Visionary Company*, 329.
17   Bloom, 334.
18   Barnard, *Shelley's Religion*, 176-7.

is a hymn to the oneness of life infused with love. First, Choruses of Hours and Spirits sing a tribute to Wisdom and Will which have enabled man to escape from the tyranny of history, and which in the future will enable him to build an ordered anarchy out of chaos.[19]

> We come from the mind
> Of human kind,
> Which was late so dusk, and obscene, and blind;
> Now 'tis an ocean
> Of clear emotion,
> A heaven of serene and mighty motion.
> . . . .
> And our singing shall build
> In the void's loose field
> A world for the Spirit of Wisdom to wield;
> We will take our plan
> From the new world of man
> And our work shall be called the Promethean.
> . . . .
> We whirl, singing loud, round the gathering sphere,
> Till the trees, and the beasts, and the clouds appear
> From its chaos made calm by love not fear.
>
> (IV, 93–8, 153–8, 169–71)

Second, the Earth and the Moon sing a tribute to Love which has enabled man to fulfill himself in time, and which in the future will create the passionate energy necessary for perpetual renewal.[20]

> Man, one harmonious soul of many a soul,
> Whose nature is its own divine control,
> Where all things flow to all, as rivers to the sea;
> Familiar acts are beautiful through love;
> Labour, and pain, and grief, in life's green grove
> Sport like tame beasts, none knew how gentle they could be!
>
> (IV, 400–5)

And in conclusion, Demogorgon sings his vision of revolution and reality.

[19] "The ideally non-violent state will be an ordered anarchy" (Mahatma Gandhi, *Gandhi On Non-Violence*, 55).
[20] "Life to me would lose all its interest if I felt that I could not attain perfect love on earth. After all, what matters is that our capacity for loving ever expands" (Mahatma Gandhi, as quoted by Erikson, *Gandhi's Truth*, 316).

Gentleness, Virtue, Wisdom, and Endurance,
These are the seals of that most firm assurance
   Which bars the pit over Destruction's strength;
And if, with infirm hand, Eternity,
Mother of many acts and hours, should free
   The serpent that would clasp her with his length;
These are the spells by which to reassume
An empire o'er the disentangled doom.

(IV, 562–9)

Love and Wisdom have combined with the will of man to overthrow "Heaven's despotism", and they are even now folding
their healing wings over the world (IV, 554-61). But, in the future,
if evil, which is eternal, should again win supremacy in the world
of man, "Gentleness, Virtue, Wisdom, and Endurance" will
assure man victory. Shelley asserts, through Demogorgon, that
man has the innate ability to control the quality of his life. His
will is free.

The final lyric of the poem was later adopted by a Punjabi
student at the time of the Calcutta student strike in 1921 (an anti-
British movement of non-cooperation) as a motto for *Satyagraha*.
The aptness of Shelley's song to the nonviolent movement in India evidently appealed to Gandhi, and he published it.[21]

To suffer woes which Hope thinks infinite;
To forgive wrongs darker than death or night;
   To defy Power, which seems omnipotent;
To love, and bear; to hope till Hope creates
From its own wreck the thing it contemplates:
   Neither to change, nor falter, nor repent;
This, like thy glory, Titan, is to be
Good, great and joyous, beautiful and free;
This is alone Life, Joy, Empire, and Victory!

(IV, 570–8)

3

The nonviolent revolution of the world begins in the mind of man.
When Prometheus, after thousands of years of torture, both physical and mental, forgives his tormentor Jupiter, this single act of

21   Ashe, *Gandhi*, 212.

the will sets in motion the chain of events that lead to Jupiter's overthrow and Prometheus' liberation. For when Prometheus begins to pity rather than hate Jupiter, he thinks of his long-separated love, Asia, in a way he has not been able to do since his fall. Asia intuitively feels the change that has come over the Titan's heart, and thus is free to seek out Demogorgon, a figure who represents eternity, necessity, that amoral force that exists outside of man, in an attempt to discover when she might be reunited with Prometheus. As a result of her meeting with Demogorgon, Asia is transformed into pure love – a force with the endurance of long suffering and the understanding of temporal experience. At the moment of Jupiter's overthrow by Demogorgon, she is reunited with Prometheus, and their union symbolizes the completion of the revolution of the human spirit – the poem's central concern. But Shelley makes it clear that all succeeding action is dependent upon Prometheus' voluntary choice at the beginning of the play – "I wish no living thing to suffer pain."[22] As Cameron has pointed out, "Demogorgon can overthrow the old order without the aid of Asia, but he cannot build a new one unless she assists him."[23] In other words, historical inevitability may cause the French Revolution to occur since despotism sows the seeds of its own destruction, but it will just replace one tyranny with another unless suffering love infused with forgiveness and wisdom combine with and in the human spirit to form an active force to establish the reign of peace and brotherhood. This, in general terms, is what I take to be the philosophical meaning of *Prometheus Unbound* as derived from its basic plot structure. And despite a sometimes radical shift in focus, it is the fundamental philosophical core of all Shelley's writings. It is at the core of *The Cenci*, the principal subject of our next chapter.

[22] As Mahatma Gandhi has written: "There is no love where there is no will" (As quoted by Erikson, 290).
[23] "Political Symbolism", 744.

VI

THE DRAMAS

Ye have heard that it hath been said, Thou
shalt love thy neighbor, and hate thine enemy.
But I say unto you, Love your enemies, bless
them that curse you, do good to them that hate
you, and pray for them which despitefully use
you, and persecute you.

Matthew 5:43-44

The revolutionary has no other choice in
love than to seek with his whole being a new
heaven and a new earth. Anything less is an
infidelity to the suffering family of man and
to his own vision born of crisis.

James W. Douglas

To the end of his life, Shelley held a firm belief that man through
an imaginative comprehension of nonviolence could improve his
condition on earth – could bring the reality closer to the dream.
His later works examine the problem of violence, hate, and revenge in human behavior, as well as man's need for love, and the
glory and beauty of love fulfilled. As an artist Shelley had matured
considerably from the days of his self-assured railing and moral-
izing in *Queen Mab*. Throughout his poetic career Shelley remained unchanged in his sympathy for the oppressed and in his
opposition to the oppressors, but in the artistic presentation of his
vision Shelley frequently examined from different perspectives
what he considered the central dynamic reality in human existence
– the struggle between good and evil, love and hate. In this and
the following chapter we will briefly survey some of Shelley's remaining works to discover how Shelley's diverse artistic com-
positions served to enrich and deepen his own understanding of

the nonviolent promise and the readers' imaginative identification with it. One of the primary reasons for Shelley's conscious experimentation with various literary forms was his desire to communicate to more people his vision of truth. In this chapter we will consider Shelley's drama *The Cenci* (which Shelley wrote after he completed the third act and before he began the fourth act of *Prometheus Unbound*) as well as his other dramas *Swellfoot the Tyrant, Hellas,* and *Charles I,* a dramatic fragment Shelley left unfinished at the time of his death.

THE CENCI

At first glance the differences both in form and subject matter between *Prometheus Unbound* and *The Cenci* appear so remarkable that it seems improbable that they could be written by the same author at roughly the same time. The former, as we have seen, is a lyrical drama of an idealistic mind which concludes by glorifying the apocalypse of love fulfilled and man's potential realized, while the latter is a "serious" drama of a "sad reality" which concludes with the deaths of the oppressor and the oppressed and no fundamental change in the world of men. However, as numerous commentators have noticed,[1] the subject matter of the two dramas is basically the same; Shelley simply has radically shifted his artistic focus. On the most obvious level *The Cenci* like *Prometheus Unbound* and *The Revolt of Islam* is about the eternal conflict between good and evil. Count Cenci resembles Jupiter and Beatrice resembles Prometheus – the resolutions of the two plays are different because Beatrice chooses to fulfill her hate through revenge, while Prometheus chooses to fulfill his love through will. Beatrice's murder of her father inevitably admits her sensitive nature into the historical cycle of evil responding to evil, and once she submits to the efficacy of revenge she is destroyed as she destroys. Before her hate blinds her to wisdom, Beatrice herself in Act I has said that "ill must come of ill" (I, iii,

---

[1] For example, see Woodring, *Politics in English Romantic Poetry,* 310-11, and Stovall, *Desire and Restraint in Shelley,* 250-51.

151). While Prometheus was triumphant, Beatrice was tragic, for as Roland Duerksen has said, she was "unable to free herself – unable to translate into actual practice on the human scale the Promethean act of liberation through boundless love".[2]

The plot of *The Cenci* is well known and need not be elaborately rehearsed here. Count Cenci, one of the most evil and violent characters ever conceived, hates all living things, and especially his family. Beatrice, his daughter, because she is innocent and pure, he particularly hates. He is allowed to commit murderous crimes again and again because the Pope is corrupt and allows Cenci to materially enrich the papal coffers in return for amnesty, and because the Pope respects the tyranny of parents as an analogous foundation to his own despotism. Because Beatrice is hateful to him the Count decides to destroy her, body and soul, by incestuously forcing himself upon her. After the crime is committed, Beatrice, with the aid of her step-mother, Lucretia, her brother Giacomo, her ill-advised confidant Orsino, and two hired killers, Marzio and Olimpio, murders Cenci in his sleep. Immediately after the act of vengeance, Savella, the papal legate, arrives and arrests the guilty parties (Orsino escapes). At the end Giacomo and Lucretia confess to the crime, while Beatrice vehemently denies her guilt. All are executed.

While the details of the plot are generally agreed upon by Shelley scholars, the value of the drama is not, nor is there any generally agreed upon interpretation of its meaning. Among modern critics, Newman Ivey White has led the way in proclaiming that "the play is far less suitable to the theatre than Shelley supposed",[3] and Stuart Curran has countered in his recent study with the opinion that the play is "clearly a stageworthy drama".[4] The range of critical interpretation is just as diffuse. Carl Grabo states that in *The Cenci* Shelley "seems to say that there are experiences too harsh to be endured, wrongs which can humanly be answered only by wrong".[5] Stuart Curran is even more emphatic: "the trag-

---

[2]   *Cenci*, viii.
[3]   *Shelley*, II, 140.
[4]   *Shelley's Cenci* (Princeton: Princeton University Press, 1970), 255-6.
[5]   *The Magic Plant*, 303.

edy is that good is helpless to combat evil, that the overwhelming wickedness of Cenci and the society supporting him destroys the foundations on which the good and noble depend for strength".[6] On the other hand, scholars such as Ellsworth Barnard, Carl Woodring, and Roland Duerksen see the play as an affirmation of Shelley's belief that men should not return evil for evil.[7] As Woodring states: "Not even in the fiendish despotism that oppressed Beatrice is violence a fit return for injury".[8]

This dichotomy of interpretation arises from Shelley's obvious sympathy with his heroine even after she has committed her crime of vengeance. However, sympathy with the heroine and sympathy with her crime are two different things. As Shelley points out in his "Preface", – "Revenge, retaliation, atonement, are pernicious mistakes. If Beatrice had thought in this manner she would have been wiser and better; but she would not have been a tragic character" (II, 71). Because of Shelley's desire to disseminate and glorify the good and beautiful in existence, he has often in earlier writings failed to depict credibly the pernicious reality of evil to individual lives. But because of his developing awareness in philosophical nonviolence, he can now turn to a "realistic" situation of man implicated in and surrounded by evil. Shelley does this not only in *The Cenci,* but in *Hellas* and *Charles I* as well. It is not only in the "Preface" to *The Cenci* and in his letters concerning the play[9] that we can learn Shelley's meaning, but in the way he has drawn Beatrice Cenci.

One of the contentions of critics who believe that the story of Beatrice led Shelley to realize that some kinds of evil left man no alternative but to return violence with violence is the fact that his heroine is conceived as such a morally grand character. In other words, if anyone could surmount evil through peace and love it would be she. Thus Curran writes that "There is no tragic 'flaw' in Shelley's play",[10] and Newman Ivey White asserts,

---

[6] *Shelley's Cenci,* 259.
[7] Barnard, *Shelley's Religion,* 133-4; Woodring, *Politics in English Romantic Poetry* 313; Duerksen, *Cenci,* viii-ix.
[8] Woodring, 313.
[9] See letters 499, 504, 508, 563.
[10] Curran, 259.

Yet in writing the drama Shelley is so sympathetic with his heroine that he can scarcely tolerate his own notion of revenge as a part of her character. Her real motive for the murder is self-protection and an almost religious mission to rid her family and the world of a dangerous monster. It is only by a narrow margin that she escapes the dramatic fault of being a flawless character.[11]

Beatrice Cenci is more human than some scholars think. She is as proud as she is pure, and her pride makes her blind to the moral consequences of her actions. She is indeed the daughter of her father: Shelley contrasts the purity of Beatrice with the evil of Cenci in the first half of the play, and in the second half, after Beatrice begins to plot revenge, he ironically underscores the similarities of their personalities – their pride, determination, ruthless courage, and their delusions fostered by the religious superstitions of established orthodoxy. Both Cenci and his daughter rationalize their vengeful actions in religious contexts – they both see themselves as a scourge of God. Beatrice's flaw is the classical *hubris* – the pride that blinds.[12]

In the first two acts of the play the two major characters, Count Cenci and Beatrice, are fully presented and the basic conflict of the tragedy is ominously set in motion. Count Cenci is presented at the outset as a ruthlessly evil noble who enjoys torturing and murdering people for the god-like sense of power and joy that it gives him. As a metaphysical murderer, he enjoys torturing the soul of his victim before killing the body. Almost immediately we learn "that there remains a deed to act" whose horror will be worse than anything he has done before, and which if he succeeds will be the ultimate manifestation of his evil power. We soon learn that the "deed" to be done is the incestuous rape of his daughter, and its horror will outweigh that of his murders because of the purity of his victim. Considering the fervor in the final act with which the judges on orders from the Pope torture Beatrice and her family, it may not be too unreasonable to say Cenci is a product of his society. Indeed, the very first lines of the

---

[11]   *Shelley*, II, 139.
[12]   Melvin R. Watson develops the same thesis along different lines in his article "Shelley and Tragedy: The Case of Beatrice Cenci", *Keats-Shelley Journal*, VII (1958), 13-21.

play spoken by Cardinal Camillo bespeak the conspiracy of the
establishment to deny and suppress justice:

> That matter of the murder is hushed up
> If you consent to yield his Holiness
> Your fief that lies beyond the Pincian gate.   (I, i, 1–3)

These lines ironically comment on the violent ardor of the Pope
at the end of the play to see justice done.

All the rich and powerful nobles and prelates of Rome realize
the plight of the Cenci family in the hands of the monstrous Cenci, yet because they fear for their lives, their positions, and their
wealth, they refuse to get "involved".[13] Unwittingly, they attend
the banquet that Cenci has given to celebrate the death of his sons,
and afterwards they deliberately leave Beatrice and her family to
the cruelty of the Count. After all, who are they to enter a domestic
quarrel, or to question the authority of a father to rule his own
house? To question his authority would be to question their own
– and the courage to do this is usually lacking in men who profit
from their allegiance to an evil system. Beatrice is oppressed by
a conspiracy of fathers – Jehovah, the father in heaven, the Pope,
the father on earth, the citizens, the fathers of society, and Cenci,
the father of his family. Thus when Beatrice pleads for mercy for
herself and her family before the assembled guests, Cenci threatens them,

> I hope my good friends here
> Will think of their own daughters — or perhaps
> Of their own throats — before they lend an ear
> To this wild girl.   (I, iii, 129–32)

And when he attempts to get Beatrice to acquiesce in their incestuous relationship in order to kill her soul, his argument is based
on church dogma concerning filial obedience.

> She shall become (for what she most abhors
> Shall have a fascination to entrap
> Her loathing will) to her own conscious self
> All she appears to others; and when dead,
> As she shall die unshrived and unforgiven,
> A rebel to her father and her God.   (IV, i, 85–90)

[13] Duerksen, *Cenci*, xi. "Shelley realized that without the acquiescence on
the part of its subjects, despotism cannot flourish."

To disobey her father on earth is to disobey her father in heaven. Thus according to Cenci's twisted orthodoxy she is damned if she does and damned if she doesn't. Her salvation lies in the alternative Cenci does not consider – rebellion to patriarchal orthodoxy. Cenci believes that his unnatural power to have his curses come true derives from the fact that God the father in heaven responds to a father's wishes on earth. He sees himself as a scourge of God:

> That done,
> My soul, which is a scourge, will I resign
> Into the hands of him who wielded it. (IV, i, 62-4)

On the other hand, Beatrice at the beginning of the play is portrayed as a foil to Cenci. She has returned good for the evil of her father (I, iii, 111-20), but the failure of these actions to produce the desired results (indeed they increase Cenci's wrath) leads her to consider various forms of escape. She petitions the Pope (although the double-dealing Orsino never delivers the petition) and she pleads to Camillo and the other guests to remove her from her father's house. She even considers suicide (II, i, 53-7). Beatrice has endured much suffering and is near despair; she feels that she can't endure much more.

Therefore at the beginning of Act III, after Cenci has forced himself upon her, she quickly considers revenge. Though she is willing to rebel violently against her father and Jehovah's dictum concerning filial obedience, she ironically submits to their cyclical ethics of an eye-for-an-eye-for-an-eye-for-an-eye justice which ends in total blindness for everyone.[14]

> Ay, something must be done;
> What, yet I know not ... something which shall make
> The thing that I have suffered by a shadow
> In the dread lightning which avenges it. (III, i, 86-9)

Beatrice believes herself permanently marked in body and soul because of Cenci's act. Shelley had written in the "Preface": "Undoubtedly, no person can be truly dishonoured by the act of another; and the fit return to make to the most enormous injuries

---

14 I am indebted to Louis Fischer for the phrasing of this concept, *The Life of Mahatma Gandhi*, 84.

is kindness and forbearance, and a resolution to convert the in-
jurer from his dark passions by peace and love" (II, 71). But Beatrice believes herself truly dishonored; her pride is offended. When
Orsino advises her to "Accuse him of the deed, and let the law /
Avenge thee" (III, i, 152-3), her immediate response is,

> Oh, ice-hearted counsellor!
> If I could find a word that might make known
> The crime of my destroyer; and that done,
> My tongue should, like a knife, tear out the secret
> Which cankers my heart's core; ay, lay all bare,
> So that my unpolluted fame should be
> With vilest gossips a stale-mouthed story;
> A mock, a byword, and astonishment.   (III, i, 152–60)

Beatrice's pride will not allow her to tell that which she considers
will damage her "unpolluted fame" and be mocked by gossips. Although she has been an unwilling participant in the incestuous act,
she knows the world will snicker as if she were guilty, and she cannot bear such a thought. She is not even sure herself whether she
is implicated in the guilt of the crime (III, i, 116-8). Her attitude
contrasts noticeably with Oothoon's in Blake's "Visions of the
Daughters of Albion". Oothoon is wise enough to know that Bromion's act in no way affects her essential purity (although Theotormon is not), and thus she ignores the vile whisperings of the world.
Oothoon, whose spirit is free from the chains of superstitious orthodoxy (sex is holy and not impure), realizes that he who violates
another only violates himself, for, to repeat Shelley, "no person
can be truly dishonoured by the act of another". But Beatrice's
pride has blinded her to such realization. Her desire to keep her
reputation unpolluted is a primary reason why she is driven to immediate, violent revenge (before Cenci brags about it); it is also a
primary reason why she denies her guilt in the final scene (V, iv,
145-55). Her pride refuses to allow her to feel one emotion she
has never felt – shame. Her self-assured purity has been the one
thing in a life of misery that she could glory in (notice her first
conversation with Orsino), and she will commit murder rather
than lose her reputation for innocence. The play's irony is that
her purity was not lost by Cenci's act, that she had nothing to be

ashamed of, – but that in committing murder she lost that which she sought to protect.[15]

Her father, although even more perverted, has a similar notion of pride and impurity. Thus he considers one of the most fiendish elements of Beatrice's torture to be her supposed guilt and her public defamation:

> I will drag her, step by step,
> Through infamies unheard of among men:
> She shall stand shelterless in the broad noon
> Of public scorn, for acts blazoned abroad
> One among which shall be . . . What? Canst thou guess?
>
> (IV, i, 80–4)

That Beatrice's pride is similar to her father's is reinforced after the murder, when in defending herself to Savella she states that whoever killed Cenci was a scourge of God:

> That poor wretch [Marzio]
> Who stands so pale, and trembling, and amazed,
> If it be true he murdered Cenci, was
> A sword in the right hand of justest God.
> Wherefore should I have wielded it? Unless
> The crimes which mortal tongue dare never name
> God therefore scruples to avenge. (IV, iv, 123–8)

She has simply brought Jehovah's justice to earth: "Both Earth and Heaven, consenting arbiters,/Acquit our deed" (IV, iv, 24-5).

The eradication of evil from the world, no matter what means are used, is always a worthy business. Yet when it is attempted through violence, the worthiness of well-intentioned action becomes compromised – for the act itself assures the continuation of evil. Shelley emphasizes "the fallacy of revenge" in his "Preface" and again when he deviates from his source and has Savella arrive immediately after the crime to arrest Cenci for "charges of the gravest import".[16] In the play itself Shelley dramatizes a world in which violence is the accepted method of securing justice. Indeed, the society as a whole and the rulers of church and

[15] Duerksen, *Cenci*, xi. "Cenci has degraded Beatrice's spirit so that she despairs of any response higher than a resort to the old self-defeating system of violence."
[16] White, *Shelley*, II, 139.

state in particular are not only convinced that violence, revenge, and capital punishment are rightful ways of seeing justice done, they are also convinced that it is an infallible way of arriving at certain kinds of truth – thus prisoners are tortured until they reveal the truth. Measured against the morally accepted methods of her society for combatting evil, Beatrice's actions are justified, courageous, and admirable, as was Saint Peter's violent defense of his Lord in the Garden of Gethsemane. Righteous men and women often have been driven to violence when they have witnessed innocence crucified. Thus Beatrice remains a sympathetic character even after she has killed her father. But when her actions are measured against the eternal verity of the poet's vision they cannot be condoned. Just as violence was not Christ's way, it is not Shelley's. Concerning Cenci's violent end, to say that evil sows the seeds of its own destruction is to pun on terror; concerning Beatrice's violent end, it is to give meaning to platitude.

In the final act Beatrice calmly and courageously exposes the brutality and injustice of the state-church court system of justice. She continues to be as tortured and oppressed by the authoritarian, patriarchal conspiracy as ever she was when her father was living,[17] but in destroying the only person who actually knows of her body's violation, her pride finds strength to assert her innocence. She comes to believe that anyone as pure as she conceives herself to be could not do wrong. She even convinces Marzio to accept the entire guilt of the crime himself rather than contribute to the defamation of herself and her family.

> I, alas!
> Have lived but on this earth a few sad years
> And so my lot was ordered, that a father
> First turned the moments of awakening life
> To drops, each poisoning youth's sweet hope; and then
> Stabbed with one blow my everlasting soul;
> And my untainted fame; and even that peace
> Which sleeps within the core of the heart's heart.
>
> . . . .

[17] Duerksen, Cenci, xi. "Throughout the final act, Beatrice seeks liberation from the same oppression which she has experienced earlier; the embodiment of that oppression has become a system instead of an individual."

> Think, I adjure you, what it is to slay
> The reverence living in the minds of men
> Towards our ancient house, and stainless fame!
>
> (V, ii, 118–25, 144–6)

As Count Cenci once had to murder men in order to hush up previous murders, Beatrice becomes entangled deeper and deeper in the web of evil attempting to cover up her crime. While her heroic defiance of the corrupt court system is perhaps defensible, her manipulation of Marzio is not. He becomes a scapegoat sacrificed to her pride. When Beatrice tells Marzio and the Court that her father "Stabbed with one blow my everlasting soul; / and my untainted fame", whether she is lying or not her pride has blinded her to the meaning of a pure soul. If she is lying to escape punishment through another's death, her purity is polluted, her fame tainted. If she is not lying, if she believes what she says, she has been blinded through pride in her spotless reputation into believing the gossip of the world is a meaningful statement on the state of her soul. It is perhaps a sudden realization of the moral meaning of her actions that brings forth her cry of despair when she hears the death verdict (V, iv, 47-75), and that subsequently brings forth her determination to face the cold worlds of life and death with an equally "cold" heart (V, iv, 77-89). Calm and proud she faces the executioners.

In *The Cenci* Shelley identifies with the persecuted who in their attempt to create a better life turn to violence. But despite his sympathy with suffering humanity, he maintains the perspective of a nonviolent philosopher when the struggle becomes violent. Violence in reality does not accomplish the goals of those who would better this world, and it can never be condoned morally. Yet Shelley in *The Cenci* imaginatively communicates his empathy with the suffering and frustrated men and woman who bravely and determinedly combat evil, and who through a lack of wisdom turn to violence. One of the major purposes of the drama is to move men to identification with Beatrice in order that they may reexamine their traditional response to violence.[18]

[18] *Ibid.*

OEDIPUS TYRANNUS, OR SWELLFOOT THE TYRANT

Shelley conceived the idea for *Swellfoot the Tyrant* in August, 1820, while reading poetry to a friend. The local farmers of the surrounding area had brought their pigs to town for a fair, and the clamorous noise that the pigs made as they passed under the windows suggested to Shelley a frogs' chorus in Aristophanes.[19] At the same time England and all of Europe were watching with intense interest the divorce proceedings of Queen Caroline and the soon to be coronated George IV. The proceedings in the House of Lords unleashed choice bits of royal scandal for gossips, choice bits of pompous absurdity for cartoonists and satirists, and a political leverage for the Whigs to gain support from the populace which sided with the Queen. Shelley did not share the popular enthusiasm for the Queen, but he did seize the opportunity presented by pigs squealing in the street and people squawking in England to rapidly compose what one scholar has called "the only great Aristophanic lashing comedy, fantastic and grotesque, in our language".[20]

In Act I Swellfoot, or George IV, is seen opulently boasting of his power and wealth, and, together with his henchmen from church and state, Mammon (Liverpool) and Purganax (Castlereagh), tormenting and oppressing the swine of Thebes. But the oracle has prophesied,

> "Boeotia, choose reform or civil war!
> When through the streets, instead of hare with dogs,
> A Consort Queen shall hunt a King with Hogs,
> Riding on the Ionian Minotaur."   (I, i, 116–9)

The swine have rallied behind Iona (Queen Caroline) as their potential deliverer, and the ministers of despotism realize that they must act quickly to quell this threat to their absolute authoritarianism. Besides general unrest throughout the kingdom, reports are arriving that the king's soldiers are becoming treasonous.

> What is still worse, some Sows upon the ground
> Have given the ape-guards apples, nuts, and gin,

[19] White, *Shelley*, II, 224.
[20] Seymour Reiter, *A Study of Shelley's Poetry*, 253. Reiter's analysis of *Swellfoot* is the most extensive and sympathetic that I have found.

And they all whisk their tails aloft, and cry,
    "Long live Iona! down with Swellfoot!"   (I, i, 324–7)

Since the government is committed to the "Substantial Pigs" in
their battle with the "Lean-Pigs", reform that would lessen
their substantiation is out of the question. Thus they design the
"Green Bag" scheme to hoodwink the superstitious swine into
believing Iona guilty of sin and thus undesirably ugly. In Act II
Purganax explains to the full assembly of the Public Sty that the
green bag holds a magic potion that when sprinkled over "A
woman guilty of – we all know what" (II, i, 83), will turn her into a hideous creature; but, on the other hand, if she is innocent,
it will turn her into an angel.[21] This is to be the test of Iona. The
bag, of course, is really filled "with the concentrated poison of slan-
der and sealed with the seal of Fraud".[22] Before the despots can execute their treachery, Iona empties the contents of the bag on them,
thus trapping evil in its own villainy. She then mounts on the Mino-
taur, translated John Bull, and leads the swine, transformed by the
taste of power into bulls, in pursuit of violent revenge on the
former tyrants.

Although Shelley satirically imagines the Queen victorious over
George, he does not imagine a better world because of it. He is under no illusion that the emotional clamor of public support for
Queen Caroline will produce lasting reform.[23] The Queen (Iona)
likewise is committed to despotism, and with her vengeful and
violent victory the oppressors and the oppressed have simply
changed places and the circle begins again. There is only one way
to meaningful reform – the nonviolent way. Just before the Queen
empties the contents of the Green Bag on her enemies, Shelley in-
terrupts the tone of his play for a dramatic speech from the Spirit
of Liberty to the Spirit of Famine.

                        O Famine!
    I charge thee! when thou wake the multitude,
    Thou lead them not upon the paths of blood.
    The earth did never mean her foison

[21] Castlereagh brought the written charges against Queen Caroline to
Parliament in a green bag.
[22] Guinn, *Shelley's Political Thought,* 74.
[23] Woodring, 270.

> For those who crown life's cup with poison
> Of fanatic rage and meaningless revenge —
>   But for those radiant spirits, who are still
> The standard-bearers in the van of Change.   (II, ii, 90–97)

This speech alone mars the sustained satire of *Swellfoot the Tyrant*.[24] But Shelley as a poet was always more concerned with meaning than with form,[25] and the interjection of this speech in the play does serve to criticize the violence of Iona and the liberated swine that immediately follows, and to establish the author's commitment to nonviolence as a means of reform. Yet, this play without a hero or a heroine is another perspective on political man by the mature Shelley. Violent victory gives birth to ultimate defeat.

HELLAS

Hellas was written in the autumn of 1821 at Pisa, and was dedicated to Shelley's friend Prince Mavrocordato who was then fighting against the Turks for the cause of Greek independence. The play is a lyrical drama conceived on the model of Aeschylus' *Persae*. It deals with themes that are familiar to us – Shelley's love of freedom and hatred of tyranny, his sympathy with the cause of the oppressed, and his cry that true freedom can only be achieved through a revolution of love. The poem is notable for Shelley's sympathetic study of the Turkish tyrant Mahmud, and for his refusal to propagandize an immediate victory through violence for his beloved Greece.[26]

[24] Reiter, 262-3.
[25] Thus Shelley's desire to demonstrate the evil of Beatrice's revenge in *The Cenci* leads him to strain credibility in having Savella arrive immediately after the crime to arrest Cenci. "Here the desire for dramatic irony led Shelley to make use of an unmotivated act at variance with the whole conduct of the Pope throughout the play." Ernest Sutherland Bates, *A Study of Shelley's Drama The Cenci* (New York: Columbia University Press, 1908), 49.
[26] I am in radical disagreement with Carl Woodring's recent interpretation of the poem. To Woodring, *Hellas* was "written by a would-be pacifist who has now chosen to praise 'wars and fightings.' Pacificism turns out to have been a limiting rule of reason" (316). *Hellas* demonstrates that Shelley has accepted "violence as the means of securing independence" (317).

The play opens with a chorus of Greek slaves wailing their oppression, and their cries awaken the uneasily slumbering Mahmud.

> Man the Seraglio-guard! make fast the gate!
> What! from a cannonade of three short hours?
> 'Tis false! that breach towards the Bosphorus
> Cannot be practicable yet — who stirs?
>
> (114–7)

Mahmud has been experiencing a nightmare, one that he will continue to experience even though awake. Because he is a slave-master he lives in constant fear for his life, and because he is an emperor he lives in constant fear of losing his power. His suffering, although mental, is as great as that of those he enslaves. And because he is an intelligent man, he has begun to examine the meaning and purpose of his life and his emperorship, and this has led to severe doubts concerning the future of his rule. Mahmud begins to be aware of the trap of history. He sends for the wise old Jew, Ahasuerus, to answer his questions on time and change.

In the next sequence of events Mahmud receives a series of four messengers telling of the increasing momentum and success of the Greek revolutionaries. The second messenger speaks,

> Nauplia, Tripolizza, Mothon, Athens,
> Navarin, Artas, Monembasia,
> Corinth and Thebes are carried by assault,
> And every Islamite who made his dogs
> Fat with the flesh of Galilean slaves
> Passed at the edge of the sword: the lust of blood
> Which made our warriors drunk, is quenched in death;
> But like a fiery plague breaks out anew
> In deeds which make the Christian cause look pale
> In its own light.
>
> (546–55)

The Christian Greeks are every bit as bloody as the pagan Turks; they do not hesitate to engage in the revenge ethic. And while Shelley admires the courage of the rebels (373–450), he condemns the violence with which men traditionally define their bravery. Shelley can be sympathetic to the Greeks and their cause, and yet recognize the pattern of the French Revolution in their actions. People

enslaved for centuries under vicious tyrants at long last rebel, and
the violence of their rebellion rivals that of the despots and leads
to the defeat of hopes for lasting peace and freedom. Because
the Greeks have turned to violence, Shelley cannot foresee their
immediate victory, unless it be the short-lived victory of the Jaco-
bin idealists in France. Shelley introduces two semichoruses to re-
iterate his meaning:

> I hear! I hear!
> The crash as of an empire falling,
> The shrieks as of a people calling
> "Mercy! mercy!" — How they thrill!
> Then a shout of "kill! kill! kill!"   (723–7)

Semichorus I predicts the real outcome of the present revolution,
no matter who is the victor. It will be the death of mercy and
brotherly love to the glory of man's inhumane revenge. Semichorus II responds with the familiar Shelleyan nonviolent truth
that violence is self-defeating.

> Revenge and Wrong bring forth their kind,
>   The foul cubs like their parents are,
> Their den is in the guilty mind,
>   And Conscience feeds them with despair.   (729–32)

Semichorus I then replies with the vision that can break the cycle
of man's inhumanity to man.

> In sacred Athens, near the fane
>   Of Wisdom, Pity's altar stood:
> Serve not the unknown God in vain,
> But pay that broken shrine again
>   Love for hate, and tears for blood.   (733–37)

In the next scene Ahasuerus presents Mahmud with a cyclical
view of history, and prophesies that because he has submitted to
history, history will destroy him.

> Wouldst thou behold the future? — ask and have!
> Knock and it shall be opened — look and lo!
> The coming age is shadowed on the past
> As on a glass.   (803–6)

> Thou wouldst cite one out of the grave to tell
> How what was born in blood must die.   (810–11)

Mahmud will be conquered as he has conquered, for the lesson
of history works both ways – men respond to violence with violence, and such violence brings reciprocal violence. The Phantom of
Mahmud II, the founder of the Turkish Empire, appears to Mahmud and provides him with the metaphysical meaning of his life
of tyranny:

> The Anarchs of the world of darkness keep
> A throne for thee, round which thine empire lies
> Boundless and mute; and for thy subjects thou,
> Like us, shalt rule the ghosts of murdered life,
> The phantoms of the powers who rule thee now —
> Mutinous passions, and conflicting fears,
> And hopes that sate themselves on dust and die! —
> Stripped of their mortal strength, as thou of thine.
> Islam must fall, but we will reign together
> Over its ruins in the world of death.   (879–88)

There is no salvation for the violent and tyrannical who have
chosen to lock themselves in the cycles of history. Necessity demands that constantly,

> Worlds and worlds are rolling ever
> From creation to decay,   (197–8)

and only

> > Thought
> Alone, and its quick elements, Will, Passion,
> Reason, Imagination, cannot die.   (795–7)

Mahmud, like Ozymandias, has staked his immortality on his
temporal glory and power, and time is a fickle guardian. The Phantom prophesies the eventual death of the Turkish Empire and thus
to Mahmud's fame, and Mahmud perceives the truth of his existence and despairs at the moment of the Turkish cry of victory.

> > > Come what may,
> The Future must become the past, and I
> As they were to whom once this present hour,
> This gloomy crag of time to which I cling,
> Seemed an Elysian isle of peace and joy
> Never to be attained. — I must rebuke
> This drunkenness of triumph ere it die,
> And dying, bring despair. Victory! poor slaves! (923–30)

Mahmuds' last words in the drama demonstrate that he perceives
the futility of the "victory" cry. Both the Turks and the Greeks
are the "slaves" of history, of the established pattern of human
behavior that brings "woe to all! / Woe to the wronged and the
avenger" (893-4). He despairs because he can see no salvation.
But the poem's final chorus presents the poet's vision of hope.

> Oh, write no more the tale of Troy,
>   If earth Death's scroll must be!
> Nor mix with Laian rage the joy
>   Which dawns upon the free:
> Although a subtler Sphinx renew
> Riddles of death Thebes never knew.
>
> Another Athens shall arise,
>   And to remoter time
> Bequeath, like sunset to the skies,
>   The splendour of its prime;
> And leave, if nought so bright may live,
> All earth can take or Heaven can give.
>
> Saturn and Love their long repose
>   Shall burst, more bright and good
> Than all who fell, than One who rose,
>   Than many unsubdued:
> Not gold, not blood, their altar dowers,
> But votive tears and symbol flowers.
>
> Oh cease! must hate and death return?
>   Cease! must men kill and die?
> Cease! drain not to its dregs the urn
>   Of bitter prophecy.
> The world is weary of the past,
> Oh, might it die or rest at last!   (1078–1101)

In the "world's great age" of the "golden years return", the
death and violence of "the tale of Troy" must be vanquished.
The new Greece and the new world can only establish its ideals of
peace and brotherhood by escaping from the past through the
"tears" of sympathy and the "flowers" of love.

CHARLES I

Charles I was to be a "serious" historical drama. Shelley completed only a fragment of the play, but we will briefly examine it for the contribution it makes to our awareness of the artist's changing perspectives on familiar Shelleyan themes. Undoubtedly, since *Charles I* was to have been a "realistic" historical play, it was to have been a play without the familiar Shelleyan "ideal" hero. Shelley was by nature unsympathetic to the tyranny of kings and bishops, as well as to the dogmatism of puritans. He would have been sympathetic to the oppressed puritans, and unsympathetic to their cause of counter oppression. Shelley also was against capital punishment in particular and violence in general. Violence, of course, was the accepted standard of action for both the royalists and the puritans; and without tampering with history, in *Charles I* Shelley could dramatize violence begetting violence, could dramatize one evil succeeding another. Shelley thought that the final years of Charles' reign had specific parallels to England after Waterloo, and he planned to portray subtly these similarities in order to have his historical drama contain additional relevance for a contemporary audience.[27]

In the fragment that we have of the play, Shelley is working out psychological motivation in Charles and establishing tension for the coming conflict. Charles is surrounded by "knowledge-able" advisors who give him "practical" advice. Queen Henrietta demands that he "banish weak-eyed Mercy to the weak" (ii, 127), and Strafford gives the chillingly contemporary advice (to Shelley and to us) that it is best to bargain from a position of strength (ii, 152-61). Laud gives Charles the orthodox, religious point of view. His speech is the best in the unfinished play.

> Let ample powers and new instructions be
> Sent to the High Commissioners in Scotland,
> To death, imprisonment, and confiscation,
> Add torture, add the ruin of the kindred

---

[27] Besides the fact that Shelley believed the present era in England ripe for revolution unless reform was forthcoming, we can see from the fragment the similarity of Castlereagh to Strafford, and Eldon to Laud. See Woodring's note on p. 358.

Of the offender, add the brand of infamy,
Add mutilation: and if this suffice not,
Unleash the sword and fire, that in their thirst
They may lick up that scum of schismatics.
I laugh at those weak rebels who, desiring peace,
As if those dreadful arbitrating messengers
Which play the part of God 'twixt right and wrong,
Should be let loose against the innocent sleep
Of templed cities and the smiling fields,
For some poor argument of policy
Which touches our own profit or our pride
(Where it indeed were Christian charity
To turn the cheek even to the smiter's hand):
And, when our great Redeemer, when our God,
When He who gave, accepted, and retained
Himself in propitiation of our sins,
Is scorned in His immediate ministry,
With the hazard of inestimable loss
Of all the truth and discipline which is
Salvation to the extremest generation
Of men innumerable, they talk of peace!
Such peace as Canaan found, let Scotland now:
For, by that Christ who came to bring a sword,
Not peace, upon the earth, and gave command
To His disciples at the Passover
That each should sell his robe and buy a sword, —
Once strip that minister of naked wrath,
And it shall never sleep in peace again
Till Scotland bend or break.   (ii, 227–60)

Shelley here poignantly dramatizes how "the sublime human character of Jesus Christ" is betrayed and perverted by the church establishment in order to perpetuate its power and wealth. The Jesus who replaced the amputated ear of the enemy soldier becomes the Peter who cut it off. Archbishop Laud is not only not motivated by Christian love, he is not even motivated by a genuine concern for Anglican dogmatism. Rather, he is personally affronted because the rebels "deny the apostolic power" invested in him (ii, 215-26).

Although Shelley had not further developed the plot by the time of his death, we can judiciously assume that the inevitable consequences of Charles' accepting the advice of his counselors will occur. When the puritans come to power the rationale of rule will not change, as we know from the beheading of the king and Cromwell's murderous excursion into Ireland. With his considerable interest in Quakerish thought and practice, Shelley might even have known of George Fox's imprisonment for conscientious objection under the puritans, and his plea for pacificism.

All that pretend to fight for Christ, are deceived; for his kingdom is not of this world, therefore his servants do not fight. ... Such as would revenge themselves, are out of Christ's doctrine. Such as being stricken on one cheek, would not turn the other, are out of Christ's doctrine: and such as do not love one another, nor love enemies, are out of Christ's doctrine. ...[28]

In *The Revolt of Islam* and *Prometheus Unbound* the principal focus of the author is on an "idealistic" revolution. In the four dramas we have examined in this chapter the focus is on sadly "realistic" revolutions. In each of the four works the violently oppressed respond to their oppressors with violent vengeance, and as each poem ends, no substantial change in the violence of human behavior has occurred, although in *Hellas* such a change is prophesied as a nonviolent happening in the future. The four works taken together demonstrate Shelley's maturity and versatility as an artist and his continuing commitment to nonviolence as the logical, ethical, political, and philosophical basis from which to express his reverence for life. In *The Cenci* Shelley imaginatively portrays the "sad reality" of innocence corrupted and the tragedy of human potential unfulfilled; in *Swellfoot the Tyrant* he satirically conveys the pretensions of the vengeful to build a better world through violence; in *Hellas* he empathizes with a despot in despair, an emperor who has come to realize the futility of violent oppression, but who cannot envision men breaking the chains of historical necessity; and in the unfinished *Charles I* Shelley has begun to dramatize seriously the theme he satirically presented in *Swellfoot the Tyrant* – that when violence is used in a "successful" revolution the oppressor and the oppressed simply change roles, both remaining slaves to fear. In *The Revolt of Islam* and *Prometheus Unbound* Shelley's purpose was to attract people to

[28] "The Time of My Commitment", in *The Pacifist Conscience*, 91.

nonviolence by imaginatively portraying its profundity, grandeur, beauty, and promise of Utopia; in *The Cenci, Swellfoot the Tyrant, Hellas,* and *Charles I* his purpose was to make people aware of the fallacy of revenge and the futility of violence on both the political and personal levels by dramatizing the inevitable certainty of evil producing evil.

VII

OTHER WORKS

> It seems doubtful whether civilization can stand
> another war, and it is at least thinkable that
> the way out lies through nonviolence.
>
> George Orwell

> Over the expanse of five continents throughout
> the coming years an endless struggle is going
> to be pursued between violence and friendly
> persuasion, a struggle in which, granted, the
> former has a thousand times the chances of suc-
> cess than that of the latter. But I have always
> held that, if he who bases his hopes on human
> nature is a fool, he who gives up in the face
> of circumstances is a coward. And henceforth,
> the only honourable course will be to stake
> everything on a formidable gamble: that words
> are more powerful than munitions.
>
> Albert Camus

> The choice today is no longer between violence
> and nonviolence. It is either nonviolence or
> nonexistence.
>
> Martin Luther King, Jr.

Shelley's poetic imagination shaped meaning and prophecy from
the tension arising from his realistic knowledge of human life as
it is, and his idealistic vision of human life as it could be. Life as
it existed in the first decades of the nineteenth century, according
to Shelley, was corrupt, hypocritical, selfish, tyrannical, and ob-
scene. Yet Shelley continued to believe that life is what we make it,
and that man has the potential to change the quality of his life
through love. It was his duty as a poet, he believed, to make the
people aware of their power to determine the future of the race
by persuading them to exercise their empathic imaginations to at-

tain political and spiritual truth. Such also was the purpose of the
lives of Mohandas K. Gandhi and Martin Luther King. Each of
these reformers attempted to counteract the sense of helplessness
in the brutalized masses by making them aware of their inherent
nonviolent power which could and ultimately would be victorious
over the various tyrannies which stifled them and their dreams of
fulfillment. Each of the three attempted to counteract the quiet
desperation of people tyrannized by life by making them aware
of their power to master it through self-knowledge and brotherly love. In this chapter we will briefly survey Shelley's faith in humanity's ability to achieve liberty through nonviolence as it appears in a selection of his later works.

THE MASK OF ANARCHY

On August 16, 1819, the "Peterloo" Massacre occurred. Unpro-
voked government troops stormed a crowd of 60,000 people
peacefully gathered to hear "Orator" Hunt speak on government
reform. Armed with a warrant for Hunt's arrest the troops attempted to slash their way to the podium situated in the middle of Manchester Field. Nine people were killed and at least four hundred
eighteen wounded.[1] Word of the massacre reached Shelley in early September, and by the end of the month the outraged human-
itarian had completed his poem inspired by the event – *The Mask
of Anarchy*.[2]

The first movement of the poem is the triumphant march of
King Anarchy and his followers, drunk with "the wine of desola-
tion", through England to London. Three of Anarchy's henchmen
are described in detail: Murder (Castlereagh), Fraud (Eldon), and
Hypocrisy (Sidmouth). The stanza on Fraud particularly makes
use of vivid metaphor:

> Next came Fraud, and he had on,
> Like Eldon, an ermined gown;
> His big tears, for he wept well,
> Turned to mill-stones as they fell;

[1] Reiter, *A Study of Shelley's Poetry*, 205-7.
[2] White, *Shelley*, II, 105.

> And the little children, who
> Round his feet played to and fro,
> Thinking every tear a gem,
> Had their brains knocked out by them. (14–21)

In the poem's second movement Hope lies down in calm protest before the horses of Anarchy's procession, expecting her body to be crushed by the King's cruel power, as her spirit already has been.[3] But the results of this simple act are miraculous. The image of "Active Love" arises between Hope and her foes, and puts them to flight.[4] The "prostrate multitude" then listen to a voice incite them to revolutionary nonviolence – the poem's final movement.

> "Rise like Lions after slumber
> In unvanquishable number,
> Shake your chains to earth like dew,
> Which in sleep had fallen on you —
> Ye are many — they are few." (151–5)

The facts of the situation are that the multitude has been made slaves to the tyrannical few through force and cunning. They forge the arms that oppress them and they acquiesce in despotic conspiracies such as "paper coin". Realizing the truth of their situation, they must not repeat the mistakes of the French Revolution by being vengeful and violent.

> "Then it is to feel revenge
> Fiercely thirsting to exchange
> Blood for blood — and wrong for wrong —
> Do not thus when ye are strong." (193–6)

Rather than retaliation they will find victory through education, unity, non-cooperation, civil disobedience, and passive resistance.[5]

[3] Desmond King-Hele suggests Hope's protest is an early example of the sit-down demonstration, or more correctly a lie-down demonstration ("Shelley and Nuclear Disarmament Demonstrations", *Keats-Shelley Memorial Bulletin*, XVI (1965), 39-41).
[4] The phrase "Active Love" is Woodring's, 266. The mystical apparition in the poem is not specifically defined, and interpretations of "Liberty" or "Intellectual Beauty" would be equally acceptable. It is an active, nonviolent force that resists both tyranny and counter-violence.
[5] Carlos Baker makes a significant comparison and contrast between Shelley's *The Mask of Anarchy* and *The Cenci*: "It has sometimes been

"Let a vast assembly be,
And with great solemnity
Declare with measured words that ye
Are, as God made ye, free —

"Be your strong and simple words
Keen to wound as sharpened swords,
And wide as targes let them be,
With their shade to cover ye.   (299–306)

"Let the horsemen's scimitars
Wheel and flash, like sphereless stars
Thirsting to eclipse their burning
In a sea of death and mourning.

"Stand ye calm and resolute,
Like a forest close and mute,
With folded arms and looks which are
Weapons of unvanquished war, . . .   (319–26)

"And if then the tyrants dare,
Let them ride among you there,

---

suggested that Shelley contradicted himself in urging the oppressed majority
to rise up against the few 'like lions after slumber,' only to instruct them
in the next breath not to fight. There is a certain fault in the image, as-
suredly, yet Shelley was trying to walk the ethical knife-edge which was
sharpened by his hatred of violence. To him the united popular front
seemed to make any other big stick unnecessary, and he was simply putting
into verse the conception of strength in union. The clue to his position may
be found in his remark to Hunt: 'The great thing to do is . . . to inculcate
with fervour both the right of resistance and the duty of forbearance,' a
remark which provides an extremely interesting commentary upon his
most recent tragedy. When he read with mounting indignation the packet
from Peacock in which the Manchester affair was described, and while he
awaited news of the British people's reaction to such 'bloody murderous
oppression,' he felt so much like Beatrice Cenci after her father's gross
assault that he quoted in a letter the very words he had put into her mouth
as she reeled with horror: 'Something must be done. What, yet I know not,'
If the news from England made him feel like a woman raped under the
foulest circumstances, however, he conspicuously refused to sanction the
error he had condemned in the parricidal Beatrice. The doctrine preached
in *The Masque of Anarchy* is not only the right of resistance to unendurable
oppression, a course which Beatrice had bravely followed up to the moment
of her father's assault, but also the duty of forbearance, which she had
finally, and as Shelley saw it tragically, rejected" (163-4).

Slash, and stab, and maim, and hew, —
What they like, that let them do.

"With folded arms and steady eyes,
And little fear, and less surprise
Look upon them as they slay
Till their rage has died away.

"Then they will return with shame
To the place from which they came,
And the blood thus shed will speak
In hot blushes on their cheek."   (344–55)

This is Shelley's most concise poetical statement of his belief in the ultimate power of the nonviolent many to be victorious over the violent few in an actual political situation. It is a faith too "idealistic" for some political strategists to conceive. But it was not too idealistic for Gandhi when he led the Indian independence movement. It is estimated that ten thousand Indians were murdered during the struggle while not a single Britisher was killed.[6] The consequences had the Indian revolution been violent are inestimable in comparison. The zero casualty rate among his foes is a tribute to Gandhi's determination to value his enemy's life more than his own, and as such is an affirmation of his belief in the justice of his cause as well as an affirmation of his spiritual faith in mankind's common humanity. In the interest of documenting Shelley's theory of nonviolence as depicted in *The Mask of Anarchy,* perhaps we can quote an incident from the Indian struggle for freedom where Shelley's proposal for nonviolent direct action was put into practice with remarkable success. The following article was published in the Chicago *Daily News:*

Bombay, June 21. — Heroic, bearded Sikhs, several with blood dripping from their mouths, refusing to move or even to draw their "kirpans" (sacred swords) to defend themselves from the shower of lathi blows —

Hindu women and girls dressed in orange robes of sacrifice, flinging themselves on the bridles of horses and imploring mounted police not to strike male Congress volunteers, as they were Hindus themselves —

[6] Gregg, 28.

Stretcher bearers waiting beside little islands of prostrate unflinch-
ing, immovable Satyagrahis, who had flung themselves on the ground
grouped about their women upholding the flag of Swaraj —

These were the scenes on the Maidan Esplanade, Bombay's splen-
did seafront park, where the six-day deadlock between police and
Mahatma Gandhi's followers has broken out in a bewildering brutal
and stupid yet heroic spectacle.

The scene opened at six o'clock outside the Esplanade. At the
police station facing the park some hundreds of yellow turbaned blue-
clad, bare-legged Mahratti policemen were leaning on their dreaded
bamboo lathis under the command of a score of English police sergeants in topees and cotton drill.

At 6.45, marching in good formation down the tree-lined pleasant
boulevard, came the first detachment of volunteers. This was the
ambulance unit, mostly boys and young doctors, dressed in khaki with
Red Cross badges on their arms. They marched past the waiting police
without a glance to the south side of the playing field, where they
parked their ambulances and brought out their stretchers.

It was like nurses and orderlies preparing an operating theatre.

At 7 o'clock began to come processions of white-robed volunteers
bearing red, green and white banners, singing "We will take Swaraj —
India Our Mother." At the head of each walked a tiny detachment of
women and girls dressed in orange robes, many garlanded with jas-
mine. They marched steadily on past the policemen and actually lined
up behind the stretchers.

They waited there in a long front down the boulevard for the order
to march on the field.

I shall not forget the scenes which followed. Darked-faced Mahratti
policemen in their yellow turbans marched along in column led by
English sergeants across the field toward the waiting crowd. As they
neared it the police went faster and faster. The Hindus, who may be
willing to die but dread physical pain, watched them approach with
frightened eyes. Then the police broke into a charge.

Many Hindus at once ran, fleeing down the streets — but most
stood stock still.

Crash! Whack! Whack! Whack! At last the crowd broke. Only the
orange clad women were left standing beside the prostrate figures of
crumpled men. Congress volunteer ambulances clanging bells, stretcher bearers running helter-skelter across the field. Whack! Whack!
Whack!

A minute's lull and then, with flags flying another column of volunteers marched onto the vast green field. A column of Mahrattas
marched to meet them. They clashed — a clash, a rattle, dull thuds,
then the faint-hearted ran and again there was the spectacle of the

green field dotted with a line of fallen bodies and again the same
islands of orange clad Hindu women holding up the flags of Swaraj.

And here in the center of one of these islands sat a little knot of
men, their heads bowed, submitting to a rain of lathi blows — refusing to move until on a stretcher and completely laid out. And there
were stretchers within two feet of the suffering men, waiting for them.

Then came a band of fifty Sikhs — and a heroic scene. The Sikhs,
as you know, are a fierce fighting brotherhood. As soon as he can
raise one, every man wears a beard which he curls around a cord or
ties to his ears. The Sikhs also wear their hair long like women and
curl it in a topknot under their turbans. These Sikhs were Akalis of
a fanatic religious sect. They wore the kirpan, or sacred sword.

With them were fifteen of their young girls and women. The
women also wore sacred swords, and although dressed in orange saris
like Hindu women, they wore little cotton trousers which reached to
their tiny, sandaled feet. They were pretty girls and not so loud
voiced and excited as the Hindu ladies. They simply smiled — as if they
liked danger — which they do.

One of them had her little baby, which she wanted to hold up before the police and dare them to come on. She laughed at me when
my remark was translated that it was terrible to drag a child into this.

Coming from all districts as representatives of the fighting Punjab,
these Sikhs swore they would not draw their kirpans to defend themselves, but they would not leave the field. They did not.

"Never, never, never!" they cried, to the terrific delight of their
Hindu brothers, in Swaraj. "We will never retreat. We will die, we
will!" The police hesitated before hitting the Sikhs. They asked their
women would they not please, please, leave the field.

"No!" said the women, "we will die with our men."

Mounted Indian policemen who had been galloping across the
field, whacking heads indiscriminately, came to a stymie when they
faced the little cluster of blue Akali turbans on the slender Sikh men.

"The Sikhs are brave men — how can we hit them?" It was not
fear, but respect.

But the police, determined to try to clear the field, at last rushed
around the Sikh women and began to hit the men. I stood within five
feet of a Sikh leader as he took the lathi blows. He was a short,
heavily muscled man.

The blows came — he stood straight. His turban was knocked off.
The long black hair was bared with the round topknot. He closed his
eyes as the blows fell — until at last he swayed and fell to the ground.

No other Sikhs had tried to shield him, but now, shouting their
defiance, they wiped away the blood streaming from his mouth.
Hysterical Hindus rushed to him, bearing cakes of ice to rub the

contusions over his eyes. The Sikh gave me a smile — and stood for more.

And then the police threw up their hands. "You can't go on hitting a blighter when he stands up to you like that."[7]

One can easily see why Gandhi, in his earlier struggle for Indian liberties in South Africa, quoted sections of *The Mask of Anarchy* to a large crowd gathered in commitment to nonviolence.[8] One Gandhi scholar musingly speculates that Shelley's poem was the specific source that suggested the tactics of mass civil disobedience and passive resistance to the nonviolent militarist.[9]

"A PHILOSOPHICAL VIEW OF REFORM"

In "A Philosophical View of Reform", written shortly after *The Mask of Anarchy*, Shelley explains in detail why he believes passive resistance by British citizens against their domestic oppressors and their army can succeed.[10]

Lastly, if circumstances had collected a more considerable number as at Manchester on the memorable 16th of August, if the tyrants command their troops to fire upon them or cut them down unless they disperse, he [the nonviolent patriot] will exhort them peaceably to risk the danger, and to expect without resistance the onset of the cavalry, and wait with folded arms the event of the fire of the artillery and receive with unshrinking bosoms the bayonets of the charging battalions. Men are every day persuaded to incur greater perils for a less manifest advantage. And this, not because active resistance is not justifiable when all other means shall have failed, but because in this instance temperance and courage would produce greater advantages than the most decisive victory. In the first place the soldiers are men and Englishmen, and it is not to be believed that they would massacre an unresisting multitude of their countrymen drawn up in unarmed array before them and bearing in their looks the calm, deliberate resolution to perish rather than abandon the

[7] Reported by Negley Farson; quoted by Gregg, *The Power of Nonviolence*, 26-8. Reprinted with permission from Chicago *Daily News*.
[8] Fischer, *The Life of Mahatma Gandhi*, 125-6. Mentioned by Duerksen, *Shelley: Political Writings*, xxi.
[9] Ashe, *Gandhi*, 103-5.
[10] For the composition period of "A Philosophical View of Reform", see White, *Shelley*, II, 581.

assertion of their rights. In the confusion of flight the ideas of the soldier become confused and he massacres those who fly from him by the instinct of his trade. In the struggle of conflict and resistance he is irritated by a sense of his own danger; he is flattered by an apprehension of his magnanimity in incurring it; he considers the blood of his countrymen at once the pride of his valor, the pledge of his security. He applauds himself by reflecting that these base and dishonourable motives will gain him credit among his comrades and his officers, who are animated by the same as if they were something the same. But if he should observe neither resistance nor flight he would be reduced to impotence and indecision. Thus far, his ideas were governed by the same law as those of a dog who chases a flock of sheep to the corner of a field, and keeps aloof when they make the firm parade of resistance. — But the soldier is a man and an Englishman. This unexpected reception would probably throw him back upon a recollection of the true nature of the measures of which he was made the instrument, and the enemy might be converted into the ally (VII, 48–9).

The psychology of confrontation here presented by Shelley is remarkably similar to that practiced by Gandhi at the Dharasana Salt mines and elsewhere, and disseminated to western readers by Richard B. Gregg in his admirable essay "Moral Jiu-Jitsu".

Thus nonviolent resistance acts as a sort of moral jiu-jitsu. The nonviolence and good will of the victim act in the same way that the lack of physical opposition by the user of physical jiu-jitsu, does, causing the attacker to lose his moral balance. He suddenly and unexpectedly loses the moral support which the usual violent resistance of most victims would render him. He plunges forward, as it were, into a new world of values. He feels insecure because of the novelty of the situation and his ignorance of how to handle it. He loses his poise and self-confidence. The victim not only lets the attacker come, but, as it were, pulls him forward by kindness, generosity and voluntary suffering, so that the attacker loses his moral balance. The user of nonviolent resistance, knowing what he is doing and having a more creative purpose, keeps his moral balance. He uses the leverage of a superior wisdom to subdue the rough direct force of his opponent.[11]

"A Philosophical View of Reform" was left unfinished at the time of Shelley's death, and it was not published until 1920. As Roland Duerksen has pointed out, "Had this essay been published

[11] *The Power of Nonviolence*, 44.

earlier, it might have done a great deal to remove from Shelley's image the imputation of ineffectual idealism, which has been generally attributed to him."[12] Certainly the essay is full of common sense, and many of the specific proposals for reform Shelley presented have come to pass.

As Shelley reviewed the political situation in 1819 after the Manchester massacre, he became convinced that the alternatives open to the British people that he delivered in 1817 in the "Address to the People on the Death of Princess Charlotte" had changed. At that time he had said that they had three alternatives: despotism, revolution, or reform. Because of the increased agitation for reform and the continued deafness of the ministers to the cries of the people, Shelley now recognized only the two alternatives he presented in *Swellfoot the Tyrant:* reform or civil war. More than ever Shelley was convinced that gradual reform within constitutionally established channels was the just and peaceful solution to England's maladies. In "A Philosophical View of Reform", besides grounding his proposals for reform in logical and moral reasoning, he gives concrete expression to the reforms that he believes can be beneficially and nonviolently instituted at once, and to those reforms that he believes can be gradually initiated into practice.

Those reforms that the British people and the British government should immediately institute are the abolition of slavery and the establishment of free Negro nations in the West Indies; the reform of Parliament on a more representative basis since "virtual representation" is a myth; the abolition of the national debt since it economically suppresses the poor and benefits the rich; the disbandment of the standing army which in peace time represents a threat to public security is a drain on national wealth; the abolition of sinecures, another unnecessary burden on the poor; the abolition of tithes and the making of all religions equal under the law, thus insuring economic and legal justice for all citizens; and the expansion of suffrage to the majority of the nation, thus insuring a more representative parliament.

It is interesting to note Shelley's proposals for a new suffrage system. While Shelley ardently believes "that Representative As-

[12] *Shelley: Political Writings,* xvii.

sembly called the House of Commons ought questionless to be *immediately* nominated by the great mass of the people" (VII, 43), he does not recommend universal suffrage because he believes that it would be an immature attempt at a republic. This attitude demonstrates Shelley's concern that social change be gradual, controlled, nonviolent, fruitful, and that people be educated in the processes of change, instead of being blindly confronted with them.[13] Shelley goes on to disagree with Jeremy Bentham concerning women's suffrage; he fears that it also would be immature. He also recommends that voting be done not by secret ballot, but openly to insure that nothing dishonorable occurs. This final proposal would have been practical for Shelley, but not for the English peasant and workingman of 1819, to whom a vote against landlord and manufacturer meant the loss of home and job. But this proposal, like all of his recommendations, establishes Shelley's dislike of the secretive and the clandestine. To Shelley, truth is omnipotent and must be clear and open to demonstrate its power.

Besides the specific proposals for reform that Shelley propounds, several gradual changes are implied in "A Philosophical View of Reform". First of all, the people of all nations have the right to be free from foreign tyrannical oppression, as well as from domestic

[13] Shelley's emphasis on gradualism and common sense in this essay led some of his critics to suggest that the sad realities of life had induced Shelley to compromise his idealistic vision of man's potential. For example, Amuyakumar Sen, *Studies in Shelley*, 230. "The bitter experiences of a life-time had, indisputably, clipped the wings of this great spirit and brought him down from the abstract heights of Godwinian philosophy to the cold, hard realities of life. Shelley, no longer, soared to the highest regions of idealism; he was no longer luminous with great ideals, nor radiant with high aspirations. His old assurance regarding the approach of the millennium had been crushed out of existence. His belief in the attainment of human perfection by one grand act of self-sacrifice and self-realisation was completely lost. He was now convinced that 'it is better that one object so inexpressibly great and sacred should never have been attempted than that it should be attempted and fail.' Unlike the ardent disciple of Godwin who exultantly celebrated the demolition of social and political systems in his earlier works, this worshipper of *real-politik* would fain make a compromise with his opponents." Compromise is a basic tenet of nonviolent strategy. As I attempted to show in my analysis of "An Address to the Irish People" Shelley at an early stage in his career was committed to gradual reform, political compromise, and nonviolence.

tyranny. Thus Shelley believes that the English nation should lead the way in befriending the efforts of the peoples in South America, Asia, and Europe to be independent and free. India should gradually be emancipated as well as all other foreign holdings. Spain, Greece, Italy, Germany, should all be aided in their struggles for independence. In England itself, if increased suffrage is an immediate goal, then universal suffrage is a gradual goal. All people, men and women, when properly educated in political and social theory, should have an equal vote in their destiny. He also implies that England should work toward a redistribution of wealth through gradual and peaceful economic means, such as a graduated income tax. Indubitably, Shelley's long range aspirations for England and the world are grounded on egalitarian and socialistic principles. The ultimate goal of society in Shelley's view, as in Paine's, is the elimination of all government; but Shelley is realistic enough to realize that this goal should only be actively aspired to when men are enlightened enough to deserve it. It is with these far-reaching, idealistic goals in mind that Shelley propounds his specific, practical goals.

Shelley views his proposals from a realistic perspective; he realizes that if every one of his proposals were effected instantly they would have little immediate effect in relieving the everyday suffering and misery of the people. If reforms should be begun under the existing government (as they were under the liberal Tories of the 20's), then he would welcome it. If a general reform of parliament should become a reality, then that too would signify a beginning.[14] But if the existing Parliament refuses to enact the much needed reforms, refuses to reform itself, then a civil war is inevitable. In the advent of a violent struggle Shelley will align himself with the people, as he is convinced all sensible men everywhere

[14] In the middle of November Shelley wrote to Hunt: "I fear that in England things will be carried violently by the rulers, and that they will not have learned to yield in time to the spirit of the age. The great thing to do is to hold the balance between popular impatience and tyrannical obstinacy; to inculcate with fervour both the right of resistance and the duty of forbearance. You know my principles incite me to take all the good I can get in politics, for ever aspiring to something more. I am one of those whom nothing will fully satisfy, but who am ready to be partially satisfied by all that is practicable" (530).

will, in an effort to overthrow the tyranny and oppression fostered by the Establishment.

Of especial interest to us are the specific tactics that Shelley recommends to force the uncompromising government into self-reform. The true patriot will educate the masses in the purpose of political change, petition the government, hold meetings and assemblies to discuss governmental reform, criticize the government in print and thereby test the libel laws, be non-cooperative by refusing to pay taxes, defy the government through civil disobedience, and, if the government should respond with repressive violence, passively resist. Shelley's strategy, like that of Martin Luther King in our own age, is to create an atmosphere of tension through nonviolent means in which the government will be forced to consider the grievances of the people. King writes:

Nonviolent direct action seeks to create such a crisis and foster such a tension that a community which has constantly refused to negotiate is forced to confront the issue. It seeks so to dramatize the issue that it can no longer be ignored. My citing the creation of tension as part of the work of the nonviolent-resister may sound rather shocking. But I must confess that I am not afraid of the word "tension." I have earnestly opposed violent tension, but there is a type of constructive, nonviolent tension which is necessary for growth. Just as Socrates felt that it was necessary to create a tension in the mind so that individuals could rise from the bondage of myths and half-truths to the unfettered realm of creative analysis and objective appraisal, so must we see the need for nonviolent gadflies to create the kind of tension in society that will help men rise from the dark depths of prejudice and racism to the majestic heights of understanding and brotherhood.[15]

Shelley claims that the people have the constitutional "right of insurrection" which "is derived from the employment of armed force to counteract the will of the nation" (VII, 53). Yet he pleads passionately against the people turning to this "last resort". In addition to Shelley's familiar ethical and pragmatic reasons why violence should not be used is his certain knowledge that in a civil war citizens become soldiers. And when men become soldiers the individual humanness necessary to establish peace and brotherhood vanishes.

[15] *Why We Can't Wait*, 81.

A civil war, which might be engendered by the passions attending on this mode of reform [sudden or violent change], would confirm in the mass of the nation those military habits which have been already introduced by our tyrants, and with which liberty is incompatible. From the moment that a man is a soldier, he becomes a slave. He is taught obedience; his will is no longer, which is the most sacred prerogative of man, guided by his own judgment. He is taught to despise human life and human suffering; this is the universal distinction of slaves. He is more degraded than a murderer; he is like the bloody knife which has stabbed and feels not: a murderer we may abhor and despise; a soldier is by profession, beyond abhorrence and below contempt (VII, 41).

These are strong words — words the truth of which have been once again tragically reaffirmed in the modern world by the "Mylai incident" and the subsequent trial of Lieutenant Calley.

"SONG TO THE MEN OF ENGLAND"

There still remains the problem of what Shelley calls the citizens' right to "active resistance". Although Shelley repeatedly speaks against all war, he does not hesitate to say that he will back the people if a civil war should occur in England, nor does he hesitate to sympathetically support the cause of revolution in Greece, Italy, Spain, or wherever oppressed people rise up in armed rebellion against their oppressors.[16] In one sense Shelley's poem "Song to the Men of England" dramatizes his position. The poem begins by asking a series of questions of England's men concerning why they labor and suffer so that the rich can be idle and indolent on the fruits of their toil. It then states the fact of oppression and its solution.

> The seed ye sow, another reaps;
> The wealth ye find, another keeps;
> The robes ye weave, another wears;
> The arms ye forge, another bears.

[16] Shelley wrote to Hunt in November, 1819: "We cannot hesitate which party to embrace; and whatever revolutions are to occur, though oppression should change names & names cease to be oppressions, our party will be that of liberty & of the oppre[ss]ed" (527).

Sow seed, — but let no tyrant reap;
Find wealth, — let no imposter heap;
Weave robes, — let not the idle wear;
Forge arms, — in your defence to bear.   (17–24)

Non-cooperation and civil disobedience are the nonviolent tactics Shelley once again recommends to overthrow tyranny.[17] The poem simply demands that the people stop supporting the economic despotism that oppresses them, and suggests that that despotism presently supported by others' toil will fall of its own weight. "Forge arms, – in your defence to bear", is not so much a call to fight violence with violence, as it is a shifting of perspective on a fact of political life. If you are going to forge arms, don't be silly enough to give them to the tyrant that oppresses you (as you do now), but keep them for your own defense. Yet, not to avoid the issue, Shelley appears to condone armed resistance in this poem. As we have done before, perhaps we can clarify Shelley's position on this question – one he never directly considers – by comparing it to the position of Mahatma Gandhi, who frequently and forthrightly addressed himself to the question of violence in revolution. In his essay "The Doctrine of the Sword", Gandhi wrote:

I do believe that, where there is only a choice between cowardice and violence, I would advise violence. Thus when my eldest son asked me what he should have done, had he been present when I was almost fatally assaulted in 1908, whether he should have run away and seen me killed or whether he should have used his physical force which he could and wanted to use, and defended me, I told him that it was his duty to defend me even by using violence. Hence also do I advocate training in arms for those who believe in the method of violence. I would rather have India resort to arms in order to defend her honour than that she should in a cowardly manner become or remain a helpless witness to her own dishonour.

But I believe that non-violence is infinitely superior to violence, forgiveness is more manly than punishment.[18]

---

[17] "Taken with Shelley's other declarations, this has to be interpreted as an angrily defiant and active form of civil disobedience. It advises a show of force, rather than the use of force. To end conflict, it recommends that the people's strong hand be laid on the table. It calls upon workers, not to seek the occasion of disobedience, as a challenge to law, but to be fully prepared for disobedience" (Woodring, 263).

[18] *The Pacifist Conscience*, 217.

Perhaps more to the point specifically made in Shelley's "Men of England" are Gandhi's statements:

If the capacity for non-violent self-defense is lacking, there need be no hesitation in using violent means.[19]

If the people are not ready for the exercise of the non-violence of the brave, they must be ready for the use of force in self-defense.[20]

Although we can not know for sure, I speculate that Shelley's position is similar to Gandhi's. He could actively support the cause of revolution in Greece, and yet lament that the revolutionaries were not wise and imaginative enough to see the preferability of nonviolent tactics to violent ones. Such a position may seem equivocal to some; then so be it. The distinction made here is between absolute pacifism and nonviolence. The position of the nonviolent reformer is a genuinely authentic one, based on the relativeness of an individual imagination's comprehension of absolute love -- love thy neighbor, love thy enemy. It not only takes more imaginative energy to love and to forgive than to hate and to kill, but more sublime human courage as well. But as both Shelley and Gandhi realized, men whose imaginative capabilities have been stifled and corrupted by a lifetime of ignoble slavery should not be discouraged from courageously striving after the freedom necessary for the imaginative and ethical development of the race. Nonviolence must not become a weapon of tyranny, as Christianity became, and used as a moralistic doctrine by despots to enslave the people willingly and peacefully in chains of degradation.

"LINES WRITTEN AMONG THE EUGANEAN HILLS"

"Lines Written Among the Euganean Hills" was composed in October, 1818. It is a beautiful lyric song in which the poet sensible to the circular movement of the day from morn to eve to morn, and sensible to the circular movement of history from tyranny to tyranny, individually through imaginative power breaks

19 *Gandhi On Non-Violence,* 38.
20 *Gandhi On Non-Violence,* 41.

the metaphorical circles of time that enslave him as he emotionally moves from quiet desperation to quiet exaltation. His depression arises out of his clear-sighted vision of the tragedy of historical circumstance and man's apparent inability to transcend it:

> Men must reap the things they sow,
> Force from force must ever flow,
> Or worse; but 'tis a bitter woe
> That love or reason cannot change
> The despot's rage, the slave's revenge. (231–5)

His movement to serenity arises from his increasing sense of the power of his individual imagination and will to shape an existence for himself and his loved ones, an existence that conquers the deadly cycles of human history by refusing to participate in them. Instead of submitting to life's tyranny, he perhaps can escape to

> ... some calm and blooming cove,
> Where for me, and those I love,
> May a windless bower be built
> Far from passion, pain, and guilt. (342–5)

But to such a socially-minded poet an escape to an island retreat is not a turning of his back on humanity, but an invitation for them to join him in his nonviolent Utopia.

> We may live so happy there,
> That the spirits of the air,
> Envying us, may even entice
> To our healing paradise
> The polluting multitude;
> But their rage would be subdued
> By that clime divine and calm,
> And the winds whose wings rain balm
> On the uplifted soul, and leaves
> Under which the bright sea heaves:
> While each breathless interval
> In their whisperings musical
> The inspired soul supplies
> With its own deep melodies,
> And the love which heals all strife
> Circling, like the breath of life,
> All things in that sweet abode

With its own mild brotherhood:
They, not it, would change; and soon
Every sprite beneath the moon
Would repent its envy vain,
And the earth grow young again.   (352–73)

Shelley's island retreat can become the continents of the world if
the polluting multitude would will to leave their rage and envy behind them in joyful acceptance of love and brotherhood. The poem
is not escapist, but a program of action fundamental to every nonviolent crusader – that is, to attract the timid masses to the joy
and beauty of the pacific island of nonviolence through personal
example, or, to put it another way, to be the enviable island of
love sans immigration laws in an ocean of hate.

THE TRIUMPH OF LIFE

The Triumph of Life, the unfinished last poem of Shelley, would
perhaps have contained the same basic thematic structure as
"Lines Written Among the Euganean Hills", although more elaborately developed and dramatically presented. The central image
of the poem is the Car of Life that moves without direction through
time, dragging the chained human spirits which are its victims.[21]
Only two figures, Socrates and Christ, are specifically alluded to
as among the "sacred few" to escape Life's enslaving chains. We
may assume that it is the meaning of these two men's lives, imaginatively comprehended by the poet, which will allow him to es-

[21] Shelley's vivid portrayal of the rampant evil and corruption in the world
is often interpreted by critics as constituting a waning of his idealism. However, Shelley consistently recognized the domination of evil in the lives of
most men (witness the wholesale slaughter of the Patriots at the end of his
idealistic poem *The Revolt of Islam*). A realistic recognition of the power
of evil in the world is a necessary requirement of the nonviolent reformer.
As James Douglas has said of two twentieth century figures: "The two-
sided realism of Gandhi and Pope John would affirm that all men, whether
Germans, British, or Americans, are capable of profound evil at the same
time as they remain permanently open to the redemptive power of Truth.
On the other hand, the optimism of non-violence is not a blindness to the
evil present in man but a recognition of the power of his spirit to overcome
it" (91-2).

cape Life, and that the reader's vicarious experience will allow
him to do the same – if he wills it. The meaning of the lives of Socrates and Christ, although sketchily depicted in the fragment,
nevertheless can be reasonably ascertained from the poem. We
can surmise that the central meaning of Athens is "Know Thyself", and that the central meaning of Jerusalem is "Love Thy
Neighbor As Thyself". Properly comprehended, of course, they
are encompassed in a single truth concerning humankind's self-
realization through self-annihilation – the Biblical "He who loses
his life shall find it."

What is completed of the poem justifies this analysis. The poet,
along the wayside, is fascinated by the strange, visionary spectacle of the Car of Life and its captives. Musing to himself on the
meaning of this abject situation, he is interrupted by one of the
"deluded crew", the spirit of Rousseau, who begins to explain
the meaning of the vision. He answers the poet's question: "And
who are those chained to the car?"

> "The wise,
>
> "The great, the unforgotten, — they who wore
> Mitres and helms and crowns, or wreaths of light,
> Signs of thought's empire over thought — their lore
>
> "Taught them not this, to know themselves; their might
> Could not repress the mystery within,
> And for the morn of truth they feigned, deep night
>
> "Caught them ere evening." (208–15)

Because they dedicated their lives to the world they never knew
themselves, and because they did not know themselves, life bore
them sightlessly through existence. Or as Carl Woodring has put
it: "To know yourself, then, means to avoid dominion over others, thus to escape life's dominion over you, and in the effect to
love your neighbor".[22] The people who have failed to know themselves include among others Napoleon, Voltaire, Frederick the
Great, Emperor Paul of Russia, Catherine the Great, Leopold

[22] *Politics in English Romantic Poetry*, 322.

II, Pope Gregory, Saint John, Caesar, Constantine, Aristotle, and Alexander the Great.

On the other hand, the reason for Rousseau's being chained to the Car (and apparently Plato as well) is that he loved himself more than his neighbor. Learning from an apparition (Intellectual Beauty) "How all things are transformed except Love" (476), he selfishly seeks Love. In this respect his story is similar to that of the poet's in "Alastor". The spirit of Rousseau in *The Triumph of Life* can be considered as one of those misdirected spirits categorized by Shelley in his "Preface" to "Alastor": "Among those who attempt to exist without human sympathy, the pure and tenderhearted perish through the intensity and passion of their search after its communities, when the vacancy of their spirit suddenly makes itself felt" (I, 174). The others chained to the car are: "All else, selfish, blind, and torpid . . . those unforeseeing multitudes who constitute, together with their own, the lasting misery and loneliness of the world" (I, 174).

The Triumph of Life ends with the question "Then what is life?" But we can safely assume that life for the majority of mankind is what history has shown it to be – a selfish seeking after the things of this world; that life for the misdirected few is a selfish searching after the things of another world;[23] and that life for the sacred few is self-mastery through brotherly love. The state of existence for the sacred few is not static but creative – it is a dynamic struggle against the corrupting and degrading life of the world in a continuous attempt to fully realize the sacredness of humanity. Such is the imaginative tension operating in *The Triumph of Life*. In that struggle, in that tension, lie meaning and hope for all men.

The works surveyed in this study are by no means intended to ex-

---

[23] Shelley was constantly on guard to check his own inclination to become one of the "misdirected few". In a letter of June 18, 1922, he wrote to John Gisborne concerning *Epipsychidion*: "It is an idealized history of my life and feelings. I think one is always in love with something or other; the error, and I confess it is not easy for spirits cased in flesh and blood to avoid it, consists in seeking in a mortal image the likeness of what is perhaps eternal" (715).

haust the writings of Shelley that contain the demonstrable philosophy that in the twentieth century we associate with nonviolence. Shelley's important and famous "Hymn to Intellectual Beauty" with its appeal that the poet "fear himself, and love all humankind", can be seen to contain the essential metaphysic of the nonviolent philosopher. Several of his frequently anthologized sonnets are designed to provoke an imaginative response compatible with the nonviolent spirit. "Ozymandias" indicts the vanity of men who would build an empire on power and wealth rather than on peace and love. "England in 1819" indicts the blind tyranny of kings and priests who rule by the "two-edged sword" of violence, and whose death may bring the dawning of a brighter day. "Political Greatness" emphasizes man's self-mastery as the foundation of political liberty.

> Man who man would be,
> Must rule the empire of himself; in it
> Must be supreme, establishing his throne
> On vanquished will, quelling the anarchy
> Of hopes and fear, being himself alone.   (10–14)

As we might expect, Shelley's political odes all denounce temporal powers that rule over men by fear, and prophesy the founding of political liberty when man comes to truly know himself and love all humankind. "An Ode Written October, 1819, Before the Spaniards Had Recovered Their Liberty" is a plea to the Spanish to master the passions of revenge and pride on which tyrannies are built. The famous "Ode to Liberty" is a study of history as a cycle of tyranny begetting tyranny and the enslaving of the oppressor and oppressed, and a hymn to Liberty to disjoin man from bloodshed and suffering. "Ode to Naples" is a passionate cry from the nonviolent poet to the people of Naples to put their trust in the "Great Spirit, deepest Love" in their struggle for freedom.

Shelley's prose writings, essays and letters, likewise are infused with a hatred of oppression and violence and a love of liberty and nonviolence. Such essays as "A Letter to Lord Ellenborough" (1812), "On the Punishment of Death" (1813-14?), "An Address to the People on the Death of Princess Charlotte" (1817), "Essay on Christianity" (1812-1819?), "A Proposal for Putting Reform to the Vote Throughout the Kingdom" (1817), and "A Defence of Poetry" (1821) demonstrate Shelley's life-long commitment to nonviolence and its promise of a better world. While Shelley frequently shifted his perspective in an attempt to communicate the ethical and political truths that he believed necessary for a better society, he never wavered in his trust that nonviolence, if generally accepted by the great mass of people, could and would create that society. He dedicated his life to imaginatively communicating the human grandeur of his vision.

VIII

NONVIOLENCE: THE POETRY OF LIFE

> Of the infidel Shelley we should speak in no
> compromising terms, were he still capable of
> future mischief. But he is dead, and the world
> has no more to do with him. His pernicious
> writings are the legacy he has left us – and with
> them we shall deal as freely as we would with
> the obscenities of Rochester or the impiety of
> Voltaire.
>
> Anonymous Reviewer

> In the evolution of civilization, if it is to survive,
> all men cannot fail eventually to adopt [Gan-
> dhi's] belief that the process of mass application
> of force to resolve contentious issues is funda-
> mentally not only wrong but contains within
> itself the germs of self-destruction.
> Gandhi, however, was one of those prophets
> who lived far ahead of his times.
>
> General Douglas MacArthur

The world is in need of prophets. It is in need of the empathic
imaginative power that realizes "the great secret of morals is
love". It is in need of a mass prophetic movement that sees the
future in the present, the end in the means, the divine in the human. The power and the promise of nonviolence need to be uni-
versally realized if man is to attain his historic dream of peace and
love.

In "A Defence of Poetry" Shelley writes,

But poets, or those who imagine and express this indestructible order,
are not only the authors of language and of music, of the dance and
architecture, and statuary, and painting; they are the institutors of
laws, and the founders of civil society, and the inventors of the arts

of life, and the teachers, who draw into a certain propinquity with
the beautiful and the true, that partial apprehension of the agencies
of the invisible world which is called religion. . . . Poets, according
to the circumstances of the age and nation in which they appeared,
were called, in the earlier epochs of the world, legislators, or prophets: a poet essentially comprises and unites both these characters.
For he not only beholds intensely the present as it is, and discovers
those laws according to which present things ought to be ordered, but
he beholds the future in the present, and his thoughts are the germs
of the flower and the fruit of latest time. . . . A poet participates in the
eternal, the infinite, and the one. . . . Language, colour, form, and
religious and civil habits of action, are all instruments and materials
of poetry; they may be called poetry by that figure of speech which
considers the effect as a synonyme of the cause (VII, 112–3).

The cause and the effect are one – to compose a poem is to perform a religious and civil act, and, to reverse the coin, to perform
a truth-seeking religious and civil act is to compose a poem. As
Shelley defines the term in "A Defence of Poetry", Gandhi and
Shelley himself can be considered poets of the highest caliber.

All the authors of revolutions in opinion are not only necessarily
poets as they are inventors, nor even as their words unveil the permanent analogy of things by images which participate in the life of
truth; but as their periods are harmonious and rhythmical, and contain in themselves the elements of verse; being the echo of the eternal
music (VII, 115).

In the general but most meaningful sense, what Shelley considers
poetry and what Gandhi considers nonviolence are so similar as
to be practically indistinguishable. What Shelley demands of the
poet and what Gandhi demands of the Satyagrahi correspond
analogously. The poet, first of all, must be a good man.

A poet, as he is the author to others of the highest wisdom, pleasure,
virtue and glory, so he ought personally to be the happiest, the best,
the wisest, and the most illustrious of men. . . . That he is the wisest,
the happiest, and the best, inasmuch as he is a poet, is equally in-
controvertible: the greatest Poets have been men of the most spotless
virtue . . . (VII, 138).

A poet through word and deed records in poetry "the very image of life expressed in its eternal truth" (VII, 115). Thus an act of
forgiveness and a sincere poetic expression of forgiveness are one

and the same poem. The poet's business is with the divine in man – to create "actions according to the unchangeable forms of human nature, as existing in the mind of the creator, which is itself the image of all other minds" (VII, 115). The poet's business is with the reality of man's temporal situation – a situation in the modern world in which there is "more scientific and economical knowledge than can be accommodated to the just distribution of the produce which it multiplies" (VII, 134). The poet's job, like that of the nonviolent activist, is to merge the temporal with the divine through imaginative empathy and thus give the world that which it lacks and so desperately needs. As Shelley continues,

We want the creative faculty to imagine that which we know; we want the generous impulse to act that which we imagine; we want the poetry of life: our calculations have outrun conception; we have eaten more than we can digest. The cultivation of those sciences which have enlarged the limits of the empire of men over the external world, has, for want of the poetical faculty, proportionally circumscribed those of the internal world; and man, having enslaved the elements, remains himself a slave (VII, 134).

The eternal war between God and Mammon, between good and evil, is synonymous with the eternal war between the poetic principle and the principle of self (VII, 134). Thus a poet imagines "intensely and comprehensively" and teaches all men to identify with others and the thoughts and actions of others (VII, 118). He teaches all people the power inherent in their will and imagination – a power capable of incarnating man's divinity and thus improving his temporal condition on earth. "Poets are the unacknowledged legislators of the world" (VII, 140).

Shelley is a poet-prophet of nonviolence as a philosophy of life and a philosophy of action. Shelley's works comprehend and communicate the efficacy of nonviolence as a spiritual code of human renewal and fulfillment, and as a tactical strategy for political and social reform. Nonviolence is more than a system of political thought; it is the stuff of poetry and of life. An examination of his works reveals that nonviolence is the logical, ethical, political, and philosophical basis from which Shelley derives his reverence for life.

BIBLIOGRAPHY

SHELLEY: PRIMARY SOURCES

Clark, David L., ed., *Shelley's Prose*: *or, The Trumpet of a Prophecy*, corrected edition (Albuquerque: University of New Mexico Press, 1966).

Duerksen, Roland A., ed., *The Cenci* (New York: Bobbs-Merrill Company, Inc., 1970).

—, *Shelley*: *Political Writings* (New York: Appleton-Century-Crofts, 1970).

Hutchinson, Thomas, ed., *Shelley: Poetical Works* (London: Oxford University Press, 1967).

Ingpen, Robert, and Peck, W. E., eds., *The Complete Works of Percy Bysshe Shelley*, 10 vols. (New York: Scribner's, 1926-1930).

Jones, Frederick L., ed. *The Letters of Percy Bysshe Shelley*, 2 vols. (Oxford: Clarendon Press, 1964).

SHELLEY AND HIS TIMES

Arnold, Matthew, "Shelley", *Essays in Criticism: Second Series* (London: Macmillan and Co., 1888).

Baker, Carlos, *Shelley's Major Poetry: The Fabric of a Vision* (Princeton: Princeton University Press, 1948).

Barnard, Ellsworth, *Shelley's Religion* (Minneapolis: University of Minnesota Press, 1936).

Barrell, Joseph, *Shelley and the Thought of His Time: A Study in the History of Ideas* (New Haven: Yale University Press, 1947).

Bartel, Roland, "Anti-War Sentiment in the Late Eighteenth Century", Unpublished Dissertation, Indiana University, 1951.

Bates, Ernest Sutherland, *A Study of Shelley's Drama The Cenci* (New York: Columbia University Press, 1908).

Blake, William, *Blake: Complete Writings,* ed. Geoffrey Keynes (London: Oxford University Press, 1966).

Bloom, Harold, *Shelley's Mythmaking* (New Haven: Yale University Press, 1959).

—, *The Visionary Company* (Garden City, New York: Doubleday & Company, Inc., 1961).

Blunden, Edmund, *Shelley: A Life Story* (London: Collins, 1946).

Brailsford, Henry N., *Shelley, Godwin, and Their Circle,* second edition (London: Oxford University Press, 1951).

Brinton, Clarence Crane, *The Political Ideas of English Romanticism* (London: Oxford University Press, 1926).

Browning, Robert, *An Essay on Shelley,* ed. Richard Garnett (London: Alexander Moring, 1903).

Cameron, Kenneth Neill, "The Social Philosophy of Shelley", *Sewanee Review,* L (1942), 457-466.

——, "The Political Symbolism of *Prometheus Unbound*", *Publications of the Modern Language Association,* LVIII (1943), 728-53.

——, "Shelley and the Reformers", *Journal of English Literary History,* XII (1945), 62-86.

——, *The Young Shelley: Genesis of a Radical* (New York: Macmillan, 1950).

Campell, Olwen Ward, *Shelley and the Unromantics* (London: Methuen & Co., 1924).

Curran, Stuart, *Shelley's Cenci* (Princeton: Princeton University Press, 1970).

Damm, Robert, "A Tale of Human Power: Art and Life in Shelley's Poetic Theory", Unpublished Dissertation, Miami University, Oxford, Ohio, 1970.

Damon, S. Foster, *A Blake Dictionary* (New York: E. P. Dutton & Co., Inc., 1971).

Dowden, Edward, *The Life of P. B. Shelley*, new edition (London: Kegan Paul, Trench, Trubner & Co., 1896).

Duerksen, Roland A., *Shelleyan Ideas in Victorian Literature* (The Hague: Mouton, 1966).

Eliot, T. S., "Shelley and Keats", *The Use of Criticism and the Use of Poetry* (Cambridge, Massachusetts: Harvard University Press, 1933).

Emerson, Ralph Waldo, *Emerson's Complete Works,* 12 vols. (Boston: Houghton, Mifflin and Company, 1883-93).

Frye, Northrop, *Fearful Symmetry* (Princeton: Princeton University Press, 1947).

Godwin, William, *Enquiry Concerning Political Justice and Its Influence on Morals and Happiness,* ed. F. E. L. Priestly, 3 vols. (Toronto: University of Toronto Press, 1946).

Grabo, Carl, *The Magic Plant: The Growth of Shelley's Thought* (Chapel Hill: University of North Carolina Press, 1936).

Guinn, John Pollard, *Shelley's Political Thought* (The Hague: Mouton, 1966).

Hogg, Thomas Jefferson, *The Life of Percy Bysshe Shelley* (London: Routledge & Sons, 1906).

Hughes, Arthur Montague D'Urban, *The Nascent Mind of Shelley* (Oxford: Clarendon Press, 1947).

Hunt, Leigh, *The Autobiography of Leigh Hunt,* ed. J. E. Morpurgo (London: Cresset Press, 1949).

Ingpen, Roger, *Shelley in England,* 2 vols. (Boston and New York: Houghton Mifflin, 1917).

King-Hele, Desmond, *Shelley: The Man and the Poet* (New York: Thomas Yoseloff, 1960).

——, "Erasmus Darwin's Influence on Shelley's Early Poems", *Keats-Shelley*

Memorial Bulletin, XVI (1965), 26-8.

——, "The Influence of Erasmus Darwin on Shelley", *Keats-Shelley Memorial Bulletin*, XIII (1962), 30-36.

——, "Shelley and Nuclear Disarmament Demonstrations", *Keats-Shelley Memorial Bulletin*, XVI (1965), 39-41.

Laprade, W. L., *England and the French Revolution* (Baltimore: Johns Hopkins University Press, 1909).

Lea, F. A., *Shelley and the Romantic Revolution* (Folcroft, Pennsylvania: Folcroft Press, Inc., 1969).

McNiece, Gerald, *Shelley and the Revolutionary Idea* (Cambridge, Massachusetts: Harvard University Press, 1969).

Norman, Sylva, *Flight of the Skylark: The Development of Shelley's Reputation* (Norman, Oklahoma: University of Oklahoma Press, 1954).

Peacock, Thomas Love, *Memoirs of Shelley* (London: Henry Frowde, 1909).

Pulos, C. E., *The Deep Truth: A Study of Shelley's Scepticism* (Lincoln: University of Nebraska Press, 1962).

Reiman, Donald H., *Shelley's "The Triumph of Life": A Critical Study* (Urbana: University of Illinois Press, 1965).

——, *Percy Bysshe Shelley* (New York: Twayne Publishers, Inc., 1969).

Reiter, Seymour, *A Study of Shelley's Poetry* (Albuquerque: University of New Mexico Press, 1967).

Salt, Henry S., *Percy Bysshe Shelley: Poet and Pioneer* (Port Washington, New York: Kennikat Press, 1968).

Sen, Amiyakumar, *Studies in Shelley* (Folcroft, Pennsylvania: Folcroft Press, Inc., 1969).

Smith, Goldwin, *A History of England* (New York: Scribner's, 1966).

Stovall, Floyd H., *Desire and Restraint in Shelley* (Durham: Duke University Press, 1931).

Sutherland, John, "William Blake and Nonviolence", *The Nation* (April 29, 1969), 542-44.

Swaminathan, S. R., "Possible Indian Influence on Shelley", *Keats-Shelley Memorial Bulletin*, IX (1958), 30-45.

Thompson, Francis, *Shelley* (New York: Scribner's, 1912).

Trevelyan, G. M., *British History in the Nineteenth Century and After* (New York: Harper & Row, 1966).

Walker, Stanley A., "Peterloo, Shelley and Reform", *Publications of the Modern Language Association*, XL (1925), 128-64.

Wasserman, Earl, *Shelley's Prometheus Unbound* (Baltimore: Johns Hopkins Press, 1965).

Watson, J. Steven, *The Reign of George III 1760-1815*, Vol. XII of *The Oxford History of England*, ed. G. N. Clark, 14 vols. (Oxford: Clarendon Press, 1960).

Watson, Melvin R., "Shelley and Tragedy: The Case of Beatrice Cenci", *Keats-Shelley Journal*, VII (1958), 13-21.

White, Newman Ivey, *The Unextinguished Hearth*, Durham: Duke University Press, 1938).

——, *Shelley*, 2 vols. (New York: Alfred A. Knopf, 1940).

White, R. J., ed., *Political Tracts of Wordsworth, Coleridge, and Shelley* (Cambridge: Cambridge University Press, 1953).

Woodman, Ross Greig, *The Apocalyptic Vision in the Poetry of Shelley*

(Toronto: University of Toronto Press, 1964).

Woodring, Carl, *Politics in English Romantic Poetry* (Cambridge, Massachusetts: Harvard University Press, 1970).

Woodward, E. L., *The Age of Reform 1815-1870,* Vol. XIII of *The Oxford History of England,* ed. G. N. Clark, 14 vols. (Oxford: Clarendon Press, 1938).

Wylie, Laura Johnson, "Shelley's Democracy", *Social Studies in English Literature* (Boston and New York: Houghton Mifflin Company, 1916).

GANDHI AND NONVIOLENCE

Arendt, Hannah, *On Violence* (New York: Harcourt, Brace and World, 1969).

Ashe, Geoffry, *Gandhi* (New York: Stein and Day, 1968).

Bondurant, Joan V., *Conquest of Violence: The Gandhian Philosophy of Conflict* (Los Angeles: University of California Press, 1969).

Cadoux, Cecil John, *The Early Christian Attitude Toward War* (London: Headley Brothers, 1919).

Chavez, Cesar, "Nonviolence is a Good Cause", *Fellowship* (July, 1970), 21-2.

Douglas, James W., *The Nonviolent Cross* (London: Macmillan, 1966).

Erikson, Erik H., *Gandhi's Truth: On the Origins of Militant Nonviolence* (New York: W. W. Norton & Company, Inc., 1969).

Finn, James, ed., *Protest: Pacifism & Politics* (New York: Random House, 1967).

Fischer, Louis, *The Life of Mahatma Gandhi* (New York: Collier Books, 1950).

Gandhi, Mohandas K., *An Autobiography* (Boston: Beacon Press, 1969).

——, *The Collected Works of Mahatma Gandhi,* 30 vols. (Delhi: Publications Division, Government of India, 1958 – [still in progress]).

——, *Non-Violent Resistance* (New York: Schocken Books, 1969).

Gregg, Richard B., *The Power of Nonviolence* (New York: Schocken Books, 1959).

King, Martin Luther, *Why We Can't Wait* (New York: Harper & Row, 1963).

Krishmayya, Pasupuleti Gapala, *Mahatma Gandhi and the USA* (New York: Orient and World Publications, 1949).

Lakey, George, *Nonviolent Action: How It Works* (Wallingford, Pennsylvania: Pendle Hill, 1963).

Mayer, Peter M., *The Pacifist Conscience* (Chicago: Henry Ridgeway Company, 1967).

Merton, Thomas, ed., *Gandhi On Non-Violence* (New York: New Directions, 1965).

Miller, William Robert, *Nonviolence: A Christian Interpretation* (New York: Schocken Books, 1966).

Reuther, Rosemary, " 'Love Your Enemies' as Rebellion", *Fellowship* (July, 1970), 7-8, 23, 30-1.

Sheean, Vincent, *Lead Kindly Light* (New York: Random House, 1949).

Sibly, Mulford Q., *The Quiet Battle* (Boston: Beacon Press, 1963).

INDEX

de proprietatibus litterarum

Dfl.

de proprietatibus litterarum

Dfl.